selections from the book of

psalms

authorized king james version

grove press
new york

with an introduction by | bono

*The Pocket Canons were originally published in the U.K. in 1998 by
Canongate Books, Ltd.*
Published simultaneously in Canada
Printed in the United States of America

FIRST AMERICAN EDITION

Copyright information is on file with the Library of Congress
ISBN 0-8021-3675-3

Design by Paddy Cramsie

Grove Press
841 Broadway
New York, NY 10003

99 00 01 02   10 9 8 7 6 5 4 3 2 1

a note about pocket canons

The Authorized King James Version of the Bible, translated between 1603 and 1611, coincided with an extraordinary flowering of English literature. This version, more than any other, and possibly more than any other work in history, has had an influence in shaping the language we speak and write today. Presenting individual books from the Bible as separate volumes, as they were originally conceived, encourages the reader to approach them as literary works in their own right.

The first twelve books in this series encompass categories as diverse as history, fiction, philosophy, love poetry, and law. Each Pocket Canon also has its own introduction, specially commissioned from an impressive range of writers, which provides a personal interpretation of the text and explores its contemporary relevance.

Bono was born (Paul David Hewson) in Dublin in 1960. At seventeen he joined the embryonic U2 with three school friends. U2 released their first record with Island Records in April 1980 and have gone on to sell 87 million albums worldwide, gathering seven Grammies in the U.S. and five Brit Awards in the U.K. along the way. In 1992 their ground-breaking Zoo TV tour was hailed as the most innovative spectacle ever staged. The follow-up, 1997's Pop-Mart tour, built on that inventiveness, and played to a record-breaking four million people worldwide. In 1994 Bono was invited to present the Lifetime Achievement Award to Frank Sinatra at the Grammies. He was the guest speaker at the U.K. International Year of Literature in 1995. The Million Dollar Hotel, *a film based on a story, written by Bono, is currently in production starring Mel Gibson and directed by Wim Wenders. Bono lives in Dublin with his wife and three children.*

introduction by bono

Explaining belief has always been difficult. How do you explain a love and logic at the heart of the universe when the world is so out of whack? How about the poetic versus the actual truth found in the scriptures? Has free will got *us* crucified? And what about the dodgy characters who inhabit the tome, known as the bible, who claim to hear the voice of God?

You have to be interested, but is God?

Explaining faith is impossible ... Vision over visibility ... Instinct over intellect ... A songwriter plays a chord with the faith that he will hear the next one in his head.

One of the writers of the psalms was a musician, a harp-player whose talents were required at 'the palace' as the only medicine that would still the demons of the moody and insecure King Saul of Israel; a thought that still inspires, if not quite explaining Marilyn singing for Kennedy, or the Spice Girls in the court of Prince Charles ...

At age 12, I was a fan of David, he felt familiar ... like a pop star could feel familiar. The words of the psalms were as poetic as they were religious and he was a star. A dramatic character, because before David could fulfil the prophecy and become the king of Israel, he had to take quite a beating. He was forced into exile and ended up in a cave in some no-name border town facing the collapse of his ego and abandonment by God. But this is where the soap opera got interesting, this is where David was said to have composed his first psalm – a blues. That's what a lot of the psalms feel like to me, the blues. Man shouting at God – 'My God, my God why hast thou forsaken me? Why art thou so far from helping me?' (Psalm 22).

I hear echoes of this holy row when un-holy bluesman Robert Johnson howls 'There's a hellhound on my trail' or Van Morrison sings 'Sometimes I feel like a motherless child'. Texas Alexander mimics the psalms in 'Justice Blues': 'I cried Lord my father, Lord eh Kingdom come. Send me back my woman, then thy will be done'. Humorous, sometimes blasphemous, the blues was backslidin' music; but by its very opposition, flattered the subject of its perfect cousin Gospel.

Abandonment, displacement, is the stuff of my favourite psalms. The Psalter may be a font of gospel music, but for me it's in his despair that the psalmist really reveals the nature of his special relationship with God. Honesty, even to the point of anger. 'How long, Lord? Wilt thou hide thyself forever?' (Psalm 89) or 'Answer me when I call' (Psalm 5).

Psalms and hymns were my first taste of inspirational music. I liked the words but I wasn't sure about the tunes – with the exception of Psalm 23, 'The Lord is my Shepherd'. I remember them as droned and chanted rather than sung. Still, in an odd way, they prepared me for the honesty of John Lennon, the baroque language of Bob Dylan and Leonard Cohen, the open throat of Al Green and Stevie Wonder – when I hear these singers, I am reconnected to a part of me I have no explanation for … my 'soul' I guess.

Words and music did for me what solid, even rigorous, religious argument could never do, they introduced me to God, not belief in God, more an experiential sense of GOD. Over art, literature, reason, the way in to my spirit was a combination of words and music. As a result the Book of *Psalms* always felt open to me and led me to the poetry of *Ecclesiastes*, the *Song of Solomon*, the book of *John* … My religion could not be fiction but it had to transcend facts. It could be mystical, but not mythical and definitely not ritual …

My mother was Protestant, my father Catholic; anywhere other than Ireland that would be unremarkable. The 'Prods' at that time had the better tunes and the Catholics had the better stage-gear. My mate Gavin Friday used to say: 'Roman Catholicism is the Glamrock of religion' with its candles and psychedelic colours … Cardinal blues, scarlets and purples, smoke bombs of incense and the ring of the little bell. The Prods were better at the bigger bells, they could afford them. In Ireland wealth and Protestantism went together; to have either, was to have collaborated with the enemy, i.e. Britain. This did not fly in our house.

After going to Mass at the top of the hill, in Finglas on the north side of Dublin, my father waited outside the little Church of Ireland chapel at the bottom of the hill, where my mother had brought her two sons …

I kept myself awake thinking of the clergyman's daughter and let my eyes dive into the cinema of the stained glass. These Christian artisans had invented the movies … light projected through colour to tell their story. In the '70s the story was 'the Troubles' and the Troubles came through the stained glass; with rocks thrown more in mischief than in anger, but the message was the same; the country was to be divided along sectarian lines. I had a foot in both camps, so my Goliath became religion itself; I began to see religion as the perversion of faith. As to the five smooth stones for the sling ... I began to see God everywhere else. In girls, fun, music, justice but still – despite the lofty King James translation – the scriptures ...

I loved these stories for the basest reasons, not just the New Testament with its mind-altering concept that God might reveal himself as a baby born in straw poverty – but even the Old Testament. These were action movies, with some hardcore men and women ... the car chases, the casualties, the blood and guts; there was very little kissing ...

David was a star, the Elvis of the bible, if we can believe the chiselling of Michelangelo (check the face – but I still can't figure out this most famous Jew's foreskin). And unusually for such a 'rock star', with his lust for power, lust for women, lust for life, he had the humility of one who knew his gift worked harder than he ever would. He even danced naked in front of his troops ... the biblical equivalent of the royal walkabout. David was definitely more performance artist than politician.

Anyway, I stopped going to churches and got myself into a different kind of religion. Don't laugh, that's what being in a rock 'n' roll band is, not pseudo-religion either ... Showbusiness is Shamanism: Music is Worship; whether it's worship of women or their designer, the world or its destroyer, whether it comes from that ancient place we call soul or simply the spinal cortex, whether the prayers are on fire with a dumb rage or dove-like desire ... the smoke goes upwards ... to God or something you replace God with ... usually yourself.

Years ago, lost for words and forty minutes of recording time left before the end of our studio time, we were still looking for a song to close our third album, *War*. We wanted to put something explicitly spiritual on the record to balance the politics and the romance of it; like Bob Marley or Marvin Gaye would. We thought about the psalms ... 'Psalm 40' ... There was some squirming. We were a very 'white' rock group, and such plundering of the scriptures was taboo for a white rock group unless it was in the 'service of Satan'. Or worse, Goth.

'Psalm 40' is interesting in that it suggests a time in which grace will replace karma, and love replace the very strict laws of Moses (i.e. fulfil them). I love that thought. David, who committed some of the most selfish as well as selfless acts, was depending on it. That the scriptures are brim full of hustlers, murderers, cowards, adulterers and mercenaries used to shock me; now it is a source of great comfort.

'40' became the closing song at U2 shows and on hundreds of occasions, literally hundreds of thousands of people of every size and shape t-shirt have shouted back the refrain, pinched from 'Psalm 6': "'How long' (to sing this song)". I had thought of it as a nagging question – pulling at the hem of an invisible deity whose presence we glimpse only when we act in love. How long ... hunger? How long ... hatred?

How long until creation grows up and the chaos of its precocious, hell-bent adolescence has been discarded? I thought it odd that the vocalising of such questions could bring such comfort; to me too.

But to get back to David, it is not clear how many, if any, of these psalms David or his son Solomon really wrote. Some scholars suggest the royals never dampened their nibs and that there was a host of Holy Ghost writers ... Who cares? I didn't buy Leiber and Stoller ... they were just his songwriters ... I bought Elvis.

the book of psalms

1 Blessed is the man that walketh not
      in the counsel of the ungodly,
nor standeth in the way of sinners,
      nor sitteth in the seat of the scornful.
2 But his delight is in the law of the Lord;
      and in his law doth he meditate day and night.
3 And he shall be like a tree planted
      by the rivers of water,
            that bringeth forth his fruit in his season;
      his leaf also shall not wither;
            and whatsoever he doeth shall prosper.
4 The ungodly are not so, but are like the chaff
      which the wind driveth away.
5 Therefore the ungodly shall not stand
      in the judgment,
            nor sinners in the congregation
      of the righteous.
6 For the Lord knoweth the way of the righteous;
      but the way of the ungodly shall perish.

2

Why do the heathen rage,
and the people imagine a vain thing?
[2] The kings of the earth set themselves, and the rulers
take counsel together, against the Lord,
and against his anointed, saying,
[3] 'Let us break their bands asunder,
and cast away their cords from us.'
[4] He that sitteth in the heavens shall laugh:
the Lord shall have them in derision.
[5] Then shall he speak unto them in his wrath,
and vex them in his sore displeasure.
[6] Yet have I set my king
upon my holy hill of Zion.
[7] I will declare the decree:
the Lord hath said unto me,
'Thou art my Son;
this day have I begotten thee.
[8] Ask of me, and I shall give thee the heathen
for thine inheritance,
and the uttermost parts of the earth
for thy possession.
[9] Thou shalt break them with a rod of iron;
thou shalt dash them in pieces
like a potter's vessel.'
[10] Be wise now therefore, O ye kings:
be instructed, ye judges of the earth.
[11] Serve the Lord with fear,
and rejoice with trembling.

¹² Kiss the Son, lest he be angry,
   and ye perish from the way,
      when his wrath is kindled but a little.
   Blessed are all they
      that put their trust in him.

4 To the chief musician on Neginoth,
   a psalm of David.

Hear me when I call, O God of my righteousness:
      thou hast enlarged me when I was in distress;
   have mercy upon me, and hear my prayer.
² O ye sons of men, how long will ye turn
   my glory into shame?
      How long will ye love vanity,
   and seek after leasing? Selah.
³ But know that the Lord hath set apart him
   that is godly for himself:
      the Lord will hear when I call unto him.
⁴ Stand in awe, and sin not:
   commune with your own heart upon your bed,
      and be still. Selah.
⁵ Offer the sacrifices of righteousness,
   and put your trust in the Lord.
⁶ There be many that say,
   'Who will shew us any good?
      Lord, lift thou up the light
   of thy countenance upon us.'

⁷Thou hast put gladness in my heart,
  more than in the time that their corn
    and their wine increased.
⁸I will both lay me down in peace, and sleep,
  for thou, Lord, only makest me dwell
    in safety.

5

To the chief musician upon Nehiloth,
  a psalm of David.

Give ear to my words, O Lord,
  consider my meditation.
²Hearken unto the voice of my cry, my King,
  and my God, for unto thee will I pray.
³My voice shalt thou hear in the morning, O Lord;
  in the morning will I direct my prayer unto thee,
    and will look up.
⁴For thou art not a God
  that hath pleasure in wickedness;
    neither shall evil dwell with thee.
⁵The foolish shall not stand in thy sight:
  thou hatest all workers of iniquity.
⁶Thou shalt destroy them that speak leasing:
  the Lord will abhor the bloody and deceitful man.
⁷But as for me, I will come into thy house
  in the multitude of thy mercy:
    and in thy fear will I worship
      toward thy holy temple.

⁸ Lead me, O Lord, in thy righteousness
>   because of mine enemies;
>>   make thy way straight before my face.
⁹ For there is no faithfulness in their mouth;
>   their inward part is very wickedness;
>>   their throat is an open sepulchre;
>   they flatter with their tongue.
¹⁰ Destroy thou them, O God;
>   let them fall by their own counsels;
>>   cast them out in the multitude
>   of their transgressions;
>>   for they have rebelled against thee.
¹¹ But let all those that put their trust in thee rejoice:
>   let them ever shout for joy,
>>   because thou defendest them:
>   let them also that love thy name
>>   be joyful in thee.
¹² For thou, Lord, wilt bless the righteous;
>   with favour wilt thou compass him
>>   as with a shield.

6

To the chief musician on Neginoth upon Sheminith,
>   a psalm of David.

O Lord, rebuke me not in thine anger,
>   neither chasten me in thy hot displeasure.
² Have mercy upon me,
>   O Lord; for I am weak:

O Lord, heal me; for my bones are vexed.
³ My soul is also sore vexed;
　　but thou, O Lord, how long?
⁴ Return, O Lord, deliver my soul:
　　oh save me for thy mercies' sake.
⁵ For in death there is no remembrance of thee:
　　in the grave who shall give thee thanks?
⁶ I am weary with my groaning;
　　all the night make I my bed to swim;
　　　I water my couch with my tears.
⁷ Mine eye is consumed because of grief;
　　it waxeth old because of all mine enemies.
⁸ Depart from me, all ye workers of iniquity;
　　for the Lord hath heard the voice of my weeping.
⁹ The Lord hath heard my supplication;
　　the Lord will receive my prayer.
¹⁰ Let all mine enemies be ashamed and sore vexed:
　　let them return and be ashamed suddenly.

8　To the chief musician upon Gittith,
　　　a psalm of David.

O Lord our Lord, how excellent is thy name
　　in all the earth,
　　　who hast set thy glory above the heavens!
² Out of the mouth of babes and sucklings hast thou
　　ordained strength because of thine enemies,
　　　that thou mightest still the enemy

and the avenger.

³ When I consider thy heavens,
the work of thy fingers, the moon and the stars,
which thou hast ordained;

⁴ what is man, that thou art mindful of him?
And the son of man, that thou visitest him?

⁵ For thou hast made him a little lower
than the angels,
and hast crowned him with glory and honour.

⁶ Thou madest him to have dominion over
the works of thy hands;
thou hast put all things under his feet:

⁷ all sheep and oxen, yea,
and the beasts of the field;

⁸ the fowl of the air, and the fish of the sea,
and whatsoever passeth through
the paths of the seas.

⁹ O Lord our Lord, how excellent is thy name
in all the earth!

15

A psalm of David.

Lord, who shall abide in thy tabernacle?
Who shall dwell in thy holy hill?

² He that walketh uprightly,
and worketh righteousness,
and speaketh the truth in his heart.

³ He that backbiteth not with his tongue,

nor doeth evil to his neighbour, nor taketh up
a reproach against his neighbour.
⁴In whose eyes a vile person is contemned;
but he honoureth them that fear the Lord.
He that sweareth to his own hurt,
and changeth not.
⁵He that putteth not out his money to usury,
nor taketh reward against the innocent.
He that doeth these things
shall never be moved.

16 Michtam of David.

Preserve me, O God, for in thee
do I put my trust.
²O my soul, thou hast said unto the Lord
Thou art my Lord: my goodness extendeth
not to thee,
³but to the saints that are in the earth,
and to the excellent,
in whom is all my delight.'
⁴Their sorrows shall be multiplied
that hasten after another god:
their drink offerings of blood will I not offer,
nor take up their names into my lips.
⁵The Lord is the portion of mine inheritance
and of my cup: thou maintainest my lot.
⁶The lines are fallen unto me in pleasant places;

yea, I have a goodly heritage.
7 I will bless the Lord, who hath given me counsel:
    my reins also instruct me in the night seasons.
8 I have set the Lord always before me:
    because he is at my right hand,
        I shall not be moved.
9 Therefore my heart is glad, and my glory rejoiceth:
    my flesh also shall rest in hope.
10 For thou wilt not leave my soul in hell;
    neither wilt thou suffer thine Holy One
        to see corruption.
11 Thou wilt shew me the path of life:
    in thy presence is fulness of joy;
        at thy right hand there are pleasures
    for evermore.

19

To the chief musician, a psalm of David.

The heavens declare the glory of God;
    and the firmament sheweth his handywork.
2 Day unto day uttereth speech,
    and night unto night sheweth knowledge.
3 There is no speech nor language,
    where their voice is not heard.
4 Their line is gone out through all the earth,
    and their words to the end of the world.
        In them hath he set a tabernacle for the sun,
5 which is as a bridegroom

coming out of his chamber,

and rejoiceth as a strong man to run a race.

[6] His going forth is from the end of the heaven,

and his circuit unto the ends of it;

and there is nothing hid

from the heat thereof.

[7] The law of the Lord is perfect, converting the soul:

the testimony of the Lord is sure,

making wise the simple.

[8] The statutes of the Lord are right,

rejoicing the heart:

the commandment of the Lord is pure,

enlightening the eyes.

[9] The fear of the Lord is clean, enduring for ever:

the judgments of the Lord are true

and righteous altogether.

[10] More to be desired are they than gold,

yea, than much fine gold:

sweeter also than honey and the honeycomb.

[11] Moreover by them is thy servant warned;

and in keeping of them there is great reward.

[12] Who can understand his errors?

Cleanse thou me from secret faults.

[13] Keep back thy servant also

from presumptuous sins;

let them not have dominion over me:

then shall I be upright, and I shall be innocent

from the great transgression.

¹⁴ Let the words of my mouth,
    and the meditation of my heart,
      be acceptable in thy sight, O Lord,
    my strength, and my redeemer.

20

To the chief musician, a psalm of David.

The Lord hear thee in the day of trouble;
    the name of the God of Jacob defend thee;
² send thee help from the sanctuary,
    and strengthen thee out of Zion;
³ remember all thy offerings,
    and accept thy burnt sacrifice; Selah.
⁴ Grant thee according to thine own heart,
    and fulfil all thy counsel.
⁵ We will rejoice in thy salvation,
    and in the name of our God
      we will set up our banners:
    the Lord fulfil all thy petitions.
⁶ Now know I that the Lord saveth his anointed;
    he will hear him from his holy heaven with the
      saving strength of his right hand.
⁷ Some trust in chariots, and some in horses;
    but we will remember the name
      of the Lord our God.
⁸ They are brought down and fallen;
    but we are risen, and stand upright.
⁹ Save, Lord: let the king hear us when we call.

22

To the chief musician upon Aijeleth Shahar,
a psalm of David.

My God, my God, why hast thou forsaken me?
Why art thou so far from helping me,
and from the words of my roaring?
2 O my God, I cry in the daytime,
but thou hearest not;
and in the night season, and am not silent.
3 But thou art holy,
O thou that inhabitest the praises of Israel.
4 Our fathers trusted in thee:
they trusted, and thou didst deliver them.
5 They cried unto thee, and were delivered:
they trusted in thee, and were not confounded.
6 But I am a worm, and no man;
a reproach of men, and despised of the people.
7 All they that see me laugh me to scorn:
they shoot out the lip, they shake the head,
saying,
8 'He trusted on the Lord that he would deliver him:
let him deliver him,
seeing he delighted in him.'
9 But thou art he that took me out of the womb:
thou didst make me hope when I was upon
my mother's breasts.
10 I was cast upon thee from the womb:
thou art my God from my mother's belly.

¹¹ Be not far from me;
>> for trouble is near; for there is none to help.
¹² Many bulls have compassed me:
>> strong bulls of Bashan have beset me round.
¹³ They gaped upon me with their mouths,
>> as a ravening and a roaring lion.
¹⁴ I am poured out like water,
>> and all my bones are out of joint:
>>> my heart is like wax; it is melted
>> in the midst of my bowels.
¹⁵ My strength is dried up like a potsherd;
>> and my tongue cleaveth to my jaws;
>>> and thou hast brought me
>> into the dust of death.
¹⁶ For dogs have compassed me:
>> the assembly of the wicked have inclosed me:
>>> they pierced my hands and my feet.
¹⁷ I may tell all my bones:
>> they look and stare upon me.
¹⁸ They part my garments among them,
>> and cast lots upon my vesture.
¹⁹ But be not thou far from me, O Lord:
>> O my strength, haste thee to help me.
²⁰ Deliver my soul from the sword;
>> my darling from the power of the dog.
²¹ Save me from the lion's mouth,
>> for thou hast heard me from the horns
>>> of the unicorns.

²²I will declare thy name unto my brethren:
  in the midst of the congregation
    will I praise thee.
²³Ye that fear the Lord, praise him;
  all ye the seed of Jacob, glorify him;
    and fear him, all ye the seed of Israel.
²⁴For he hath not despised nor abhorred
  the affliction of the afflicted;
    neither hath he hid his face from him;
  but when he cried unto him, he heard.
²⁵My praise shall be of thee
  in the great congregation:
    I will pay my vows before them
  that fear him.
²⁶The meek shall eat and be satisfied:
  they shall praise the Lord that seek him:
    your heart shall live for ever.
²⁷All the ends of the world shall remember
  and turn unto the Lord:
    and all the kindreds of the nations
  shall worship before thee.
²⁸For the kingdom is the Lord's:
  and he is the governor among the nations.
²⁹All they that be fat upon earth shall eat
  and worship: all they that go down to the dust
    shall bow before him:
  and none can keep alive his own soul.
³⁰A seed shall serve him; it shall be accounted

to the Lord for a generation.
³¹ They shall come, and shall declare
his righteousness unto a people
that shall be born, that he hath done this.

23 A psalm of David.

The Lord is my shepherd; I shall not want.
² He maketh me to lie down in green pastures:
he leadeth me beside the still waters.
³ He restoreth my soul:
he leadeth me in the paths of righteousness
for his name's sake.
⁴ Yea, though I walk
through the valley of
the shadow of death,
I will fear no evil;
for thou art with me;
thy rod and thy staff they comfort me.
⁵ Thou preparest a table before me
in the presence of mine enemies;
thou anointest my head with oil;
my cup runneth over.
⁶ Surely goodness and mercy shall follow me
all the days of my life;
and I will dwell
in the house of the Lord for ever.

24

A psalm of David.

The earth is the Lord's, and the fulness thereof;
    the world, and they that dwell therein.
² For he hath founded it upon the seas,
    and established it upon the floods.
³ Who shall ascend into the hill of the Lord?
    Or who shall stand in his holy place?
⁴ He that hath clean hands, and a pure heart;
    who hath not lifted up his soul unto vanity,
        nor sworn deceitfully.
⁵ He shall receive the blessing from the Lord,
    and righteousness from the God
        of his salvation.
⁶ This is the generation of them that seek him,
    that seek thy face, O Jacob. Selah.
⁷ Lift up your heads, O ye gates;
    and be ye lift up, ye everlasting doors;
        and the King of glory shall come in.
⁸ Who is this King of glory?
    The Lord strong and mighty,
        the Lord mighty in battle.
⁹ Lift up your heads, O ye gates;
    even lift them up, ye everlasting doors;
        and the King of glory shall come in.
¹⁰ Who is this King of glory?
    The Lord of hosts, he is the King of glory. Selah.

25

A psalm of David.

Unto thee, O Lord, do I lift up my soul.
² O my God, I trust in thee: let me not be ashamed,
　　let not mine enemies triumph over me.
³ Yea, let none that wait on thee be ashamed:
　　let them be ashamed
　　　　which transgress without cause.
⁴ Shew me thy ways, O Lord;
　　teach me thy paths.
⁵ Lead me in thy truth, and teach me:
　　for thou art the God of my salvation;
　　　　on thee do I wait all the day.
⁶ Remember, O Lord,
　　thy tender mercies and thy lovingkindnesses;
　　　　for they have been ever of old.
⁷ Remember not the sins of my youth,
　　nor my transgressions:
　　　　according to thy mercy, remember thou me
　　for thy goodness' sake, O Lord.
⁸ Good and upright is the Lord;
　　therefore will he teach sinners in the way.
⁹ The meek will he guide in judgment;
　　and the meek will he teach his way.
¹⁰ All the paths of the Lord are mercy and truth
　　unto such as keep his covenant
　　　　and his testimonies.
¹¹ For thy name's sake, O Lord,

pardon mine iniquity; for it is great.

¹² What man is he that feareth the Lord?
Him shall he teach in the way
that he shall choose.

¹³ His soul shall dwell at ease;
and his seed shall inherit the earth.

¹⁴ The secret of the Lord is with them that fear him;
and he will shew them his covenant.

¹⁵ Mine eyes are ever toward the Lord;
for he shall pluck my feet out of the net.

¹⁶ Turn thee unto me, and have mercy upon me;
for I am desolate and afflicted.

¹⁷ The troubles of my heart are enlarged:
O bring thou me out of my distresses.

¹⁸ Look upon mine affliction and my pain;
and forgive all my sins.

¹⁹ Consider mine enemies; for they are many;
and they hate me with cruel hatred.

²⁰ O keep my soul, and deliver me:
let me not be ashamed;
for I put my trust in thee.

²¹ Let integrity and uprightness preserve me;
for I wait on thee.

²² Redeem Israel, O God, out of all his troubles.

27 A psalm of David.

The Lord is my light and my salvation;

whom shall I fear?
The Lord is the strength of my life;
of whom shall I be afraid?

[2] When the wicked, even mine enemies and my foes,
came upon me to eat up my flesh,
they stumbled and fell.

[3] Though an host should encamp against me,
my heart shall not fear:
though war should rise against me,
in this will I be confident.

[4] One thing have I desired of the Lord,
that will I seek after;
that I may dwell in the house of the Lord
all the days of my life,
to behold the beauty of the Lord,
and to enquire in his temple.

[5] For in the time of trouble he shall hide me
in his pavilion:
in the secret of his tabernacle
shall he hide me;
he shall set me up upon a rock.

[6] And now shall mine head be lifted up
above mine enemies round about me:
therefore will I offer in his tabernacle
sacrifices of joy; I will sing,
yea, I will sing praises unto the Lord.

[7] Hear, O Lord, when I cry with my voice:
have mercy also upon me, and answer me.

8 When thou saidst, 'Seek ye my face',
   my heart said unto thee,
      'Thy face, Lord, will I seek.'
9 Hide not thy face far from me;
   put not thy servant away in anger:
      thou hast been my help;
   leave me not, neither forsake me,
      O God of my salvation.
10 When my father and my mother forsake me,
   then the Lord will take me up.
11 Teach me thy way, O Lord,
   and lead me in a plain path,
      because of mine enemies.
12 Deliver me not over unto the will of mine enemies:
   for false witnesses are risen up against me,
      and such as breathe out cruelty.
13 I had fainted, unless I had believed
   to see the goodness of the Lord
      in the land of the living.
14 Wait on the Lord: be of good courage,
   and he shall strengthen thine heart:
      wait, I say, on the Lord.

29

A psalm of David.

Give unto the Lord, O ye mighty,
   give unto the Lord glory and strength.
2 Give unto the Lord the glory due unto his name;

worship the Lord in the beauty of holiness.
³ The voice of the Lord is upon the waters:
   the God of glory thundereth:
      the Lord is upon many waters.
⁴ The voice of the Lord is powerful;
   the voice of the Lord is full of majesty.
⁵ The voice of the Lord breaketh the cedars;
   yea, the Lord breaketh the cedars of Lebanon.
⁶ He maketh them also to skip like a calf;
   Lebanon and Sirion like a young unicorn.
⁷ The voice of the Lord divideth the flames of fire.
⁸ The voice of the Lord shaketh the wilderness;
   the Lord shaketh the wilderness of Kadesh.
⁹ The voice of the Lord maketh the hinds to calve,
   and discovereth the forests:
      and in his temple doth every one speak
   of his glory.
¹⁰ The Lord sitteth upon the flood;
   yea, the Lord sitteth King for ever.
¹¹ The Lord will give strength unto his people;
   the Lord will bless his people with peace.

30   A psalm and song at the dedication of the house
     of David.

I will extol thee, O Lord;
   for thou hast lifted me up,
      and hast not made my foes to rejoice over me.

²O Lord my God, I cried unto thee,
   and thou hast healed me.
³O Lord, thou hast brought up my soul
      from the grave: thou hast kept me alive,
         that I should not go down to the pit.
⁴Sing unto the Lord, O ye saints of his,
      and give thanks at the remembrance
         of his holiness.
⁵For his anger endureth but a moment;
      in his favour is life:
         weeping may endure for a night,
      but joy cometh in the morning.
⁶And in my prosperity I said,
      'I shall never be moved.'
⁷Lord, by thy favour thou hast made my mountain
      to stand strong: thou didst hide thy face,
         and I was troubled.
⁸I cried to thee, O Lord;
      and unto the Lord I made supplication.
⁹What profit is there in my blood,
      when I go down to the pit?
         Shall the dust praise thee?
         Shall it declare thy truth?
¹⁰Hear, O Lord, and have mercy upon me:
      Lord, be thou my helper.
¹¹Thou hast turned for me my mourning
      into dancing:
         thou hast put off my sackcloth,

and girded me with gladness;
¹² to the end that my glory may sing praise to thee,
and not be silent.
O Lord my God,
I will give thanks unto thee for ever.

31 To the chief musician, a psalm of David.

In thee, O Lord, do I put my trust;
let me never be ashamed;
deliver me in thy righteousness.
² Bow down thine ear to me;
deliver me speedily:
be thou my strong rock,
for an house of defence to save me.
³ For thou art my rock and my fortress;
therefore for thy name's sake lead me,
and guide me.
⁴ Pull me out of the net that they have laid
privily for me; for thou art my strength.
⁵ Into thine hand I commit my spirit:
thou hast redeemed me, O Lord God of truth.
⁶ I have hated them that regard lying vanities;
but I trust in the Lord.
⁷ I will be glad and rejoice in thy mercy;
for thou hast considered my trouble;
thou hast known my soul in adversities,
⁸ and hast not shut me up into the hand of the enemy:

thou hast set my feet in a large room.
⁹ Have mercy upon me, O Lord,
for I am in trouble:
mine eye is consumed with grief,
yea, my soul and my belly.
¹⁰ For my life is spent with grief,
and my years with sighing:
my strength faileth because of mine iniquity,
and my bones are consumed.
¹¹ I was a reproach among all mine enemies,
but especially among my neighbours,
and a fear to mine acquaintance:
they that did see me without fled from me.
¹² I am forgotten as a dead man out of mind:
I am like a broken vessel.
¹³ For I have heard the slander of many:
fear was on every side:
while they took counsel together against me,
they devised to take away my life.
¹⁴ But I trusted in thee, O Lord:
I said, 'Thou art my God.'
¹⁵ My times are in thy hand:
deliver me from the hand of mine enemies,
and from them that persecute me.
¹⁶ Make thy face to shine upon thy servant:
save me for thy mercies' sake.
¹⁷ Let me not be ashamed, O Lord;
for I have called upon thee:

let the wicked be ashamed,
and let them be silent in the grave.
¹⁸ Let the lying lips be put to silence,
which speak grievous things proudly
and contemptuously against the righteous.
¹⁹ Oh how great is thy goodness,
which thou hast laid up for them that fear thee;
which thou hast wrought for them
that trust in thee before the sons of men!
²⁰ Thou shalt hide them in the secret of thy presence
from the pride of man:
thou shalt keep them secretly in a pavilion
from the strife of tongues.
²¹ Blessed be the Lord;
for he hath shewed me his marvellous kindness
in a strong city.
²² For I said in my haste,
'I am cut off from before thine eyes':
nevertheless thou heardest the voice
of my supplications when I cried unto thee.
²³ O love the Lord, all ye his saints;
for the Lord preserveth the faithful,
and plentifully rewardeth the proud doer.
²⁴ Be of good courage, and he shall strengthen
your heart, all ye that hope in the Lord.

32

A psalm of David, Maschil.

Blessed is he whose transgression is forgiven,
   whose sin is covered.
2 Blessed is the man unto whom
   the Lord imputeth not iniquity,
      and in whose spirit there is no guile.
3 When I kept silence, my bones waxed old
   through my roaring all the day long.
4 For day and night thy hand was heavy upon me:
   my moisture is turned
      into the drought of summer. Selah.
5 I acknowledged my sin unto thee,
   and mine iniquity have I not hid.
      I said, 'I will confess my transgressions
   unto the Lord'; and thou forgavest the iniquity
      of my sin. Selah.
6 For this shall every one that is godly pray
   unto thee in a time when thou mayest be found:
      surely in the floods of great waters
   they shall not come nigh unto him.
7 Thou art my hiding place;
   thou shalt preserve me from trouble;
      thou shalt compass me about
   with songs of deliverance. Selah.
8 I will instruct thee and teach thee in the way
   which thou shalt go:
      I will guide thee with mine eye.

⁹ Be ye not as the horse, or as the mule,
    which have no understanding:
        whose mouth must be held in with bit
        and bridle, lest they come near unto thee.
¹⁰ Many sorrows shall be to the wicked:
    but he that trusteth in the Lord,
        mercy shall compass him about.
¹¹ Be glad in the Lord, and rejoice, ye righteous:
        and shout for joy, all ye that are upright in heart.

33 Rejoice in the Lord, O ye righteous;
    for praise is comely for the upright.
² Praise the Lord with harp:
    sing unto him with the psaltery
        and an instrument of ten strings.
³ Sing unto him a new song;
    play skilfully with a loud noise.
⁴ For the word of the Lord is right;
    and all his works are done in truth.
⁵ He loveth righteousness and judgment:
    the earth is full of the goodness of the Lord.
⁶ By the word of the Lord were the heavens made;
    and all the host of them
        by the breath of his mouth.
⁷ He gathereth the waters of the sea together
    as an heap:
        he layeth up the depth in storehouses.

⁸ Let all the earth fear the Lord:
    let all the inhabitants of the world
        stand in awe of him.
⁹ For he spake, and it was done;
    he commanded, and it stood fast.
¹⁰ The Lord bringeth the counsel of the heathen
    to nought:
        he maketh the devices of the people
    of none effect.
¹¹ The counsel of the Lord standeth for ever,
    the thoughts of his heart to all generations.
¹² Blessed is the nation whose God is the Lord;
    and the people whom he hath chosen
        for his own inheritance.
¹³ The Lord looketh from heaven;
    he beholdeth all the sons of men.
¹⁴ From the place of his habitation
    he looketh upon all the inhabitants of the earth.
¹⁵ He fashioneth their hearts alike;
    he considereth all their works.
¹⁶ There is no king saved by the multitude of an host:
    a mighty man is not delivered by much strength.
¹⁷ An horse is a vain thing for safety:
    neither shall he deliver any by his great strength.
¹⁸ Behold, the eye of the Lord is upon them that
    fear him, upon them that hope in his mercy;
¹⁹ to deliver their soul from death,
    and to keep them alive in famine.

²⁰ Our soul waiteth for the Lord:
  he is our help and our shield.
²¹ For our heart shall rejoice in him,
  because we have trusted in his holy name.
²² Let thy mercy, O Lord,
  be upon us, according as we hope in thee.

34

A psalm of David, when he changed his behaviour
before Abimelech, who drove him away,
  and he departed.

I will bless the Lord at all times:
  his praise shall continually be in my mouth.
² My soul shall make her boast in the Lord:
  the humble shall hear thereof, and be glad.
³ O magnify the Lord with me,
  and let us exalt his name together.
⁴ I sought the Lord, and he heard me,
  and delivered me from all my fears.
⁵ They looked unto him, and were lightened:
  and their faces were not ashamed.
⁶ This poor man cried, and the Lord heard him,
  and saved him out of all his troubles.
⁷ The angel of the Lord encampeth round about
  them that fear him, and delivereth them.
⁸ O taste and see that the Lord is good:
  blessed is the man that trusteth in him.
⁹ O fear the Lord, ye his saints;

for there is no want to them that fear him.

¹⁰ The young lions do lack, and suffer hunger;
but they that seek the Lord shall not want
any good thing.

¹¹ Come, ye children, hearken unto me:
I will teach you the fear of the Lord.

¹² What man is he that desireth life,
and loveth many days, that he may see good?

¹³ Keep thy tongue from evil,
and thy lips from speaking guile.

¹⁴ Depart from evil, and do good;
seek peace, and pursue it.

¹⁵ The eyes of the Lord are upon the righteous,
and his ears are open unto their cry.

¹⁶ The face of the Lord is against them that do evil,
to cut off the remembrance of them
from the earth.

¹⁷ The righteous cry, and the Lord heareth,
and delivereth them out of all their troubles.

¹⁸ The Lord is nigh unto them
that are of a broken heart;
and saveth such as be of a contrite spirit.

¹⁹ Many are the afflictions of the righteous;
but the Lord delivereth him out of them all.

²⁰ He keepeth all his bones:
not one of them is broken.

²¹ Evil shall slay the wicked:
and they that hate the righteous shall be desolate.

²² The Lord redeemeth the soul of his servants:
    and none of them that trust in him
        shall be desolate.

36

To the chief musician, a psalm of David the servant
of the Lord.

The transgression of the wicked
    saith within my heart, that there is
        no fear of God before his eyes.
² For he flattereth himself in his own eyes,
    until his iniquity be found to be hateful.
³ The words of his mouth are iniquity and deceit:
    he hath left off to be wise, and to do good.
⁴ He deviseth mischief upon his bed;
    he setteth himself in a way that is not good;
        he abhorreth not evil.
⁵ Thy mercy, O Lord, is in the heavens;
    and thy faithfulness reacheth
        unto the clouds.
⁶ Thy righteousness is like the great mountains;
    thy judgments are a great deep:
        O Lord, thou preservest man and beast.
⁷ How excellent is thy lovingkindness, O God!
    Therefore the children of men put their trust
        under the shadow of thy wings.
⁸ They shall be abundantly satisfied with the fatness
    of thy house; and thou shalt make them drink

of the river of thy pleasures.
⁹ For with thee is the fountain of life:
    in thy light shall we see light.
¹⁰ O continue thy lovingkindness
    unto them that know thee;
        and thy righteousness
    to the upright in heart.
¹¹ Let not the foot of pride come against me,
    and let not the hand of the wicked remove me.
¹² There are the workers of iniquity fallen:
    they are cast down,
        and shall not be able to rise.

37

A psalm of David.

Fret not thyself because of evildoers,
    neither be thou envious
        against the workers of iniquity.
² For they shall soon be cut down like the grass,
    and wither as the green herb.
³ Trust in the Lord, and do good;
    so shalt thou dwell in the land,
        and verily thou shalt be fed.
⁴ Delight thyself also in the Lord;
    and he shall give thee the desires of thine heart.
⁵ Commit thy way unto the Lord;
    trust also in him; and he shall bring it to pass.
⁶ And he shall bring forth thy righteousness

as the light, and thy judgment as the noonday.
⁷ Rest in the Lord, and wait patiently for him:
  fret not thyself because of him who prospereth
    in his way, because of the man who bringeth
  wicked devices to pass.
⁸ Cease from anger, and forsake wrath:
  fret not thyself in any wise to do evil.
⁹ For evildoers shall be cut off:
  but those that wait upon the Lord,
    they shall inherit the earth.
¹⁰ For yet a little while, and the wicked shall not be:
  yea, thou shalt diligently consider his place,
    and it shall not be.
¹¹ But the meek shall inherit the earth;
  and shall delight themselves
    in the abundance of peace.
¹² The wicked plotteth against the just,
  and gnasheth upon him with his teeth.
¹³ The Lord shall laugh at him:
  for he seeth that his day is coming.
¹⁴ The wicked have drawn out the sword,
  and have bent their bow,
    to cast down the poor and needy,
  and to slay such as be of upright conversation.
¹⁵ Their sword shall enter into their own heart,
  and their bows shall be broken.
¹⁶ A little that a righteous man hath
  is better than the riches of many wicked.

¹⁷ For the arms of the wicked shall be broken;
 but the Lord upholdeth the righteous.
¹⁸ The Lord knoweth the days of the upright:
 and their inheritance shall be for ever.
¹⁹ They shall not be ashamed in the evil time:
 and in the days of famine they shall be satisfied.
²⁰ But the wicked shall perish, and the enemies
 of the Lord shall be as the fat of lambs;
  they shall consume;
 into smoke shall they consume away.
²¹ The wicked borroweth, and payeth not again;
 but the righteous sheweth mercy, and giveth.
²² For such as be blessed of him shall inherit
 the earth;
  and they that be cursed of him
 shall be cut off.
²³ The steps of a good man are ordered by the Lord,
 and he delighteth in his way.
²⁴ Though he fall, he shall not be utterly cast down;
 for the Lord upholdeth him with his hand.
²⁵ I have been young, and now am old;
 yet have I not seen the righteous forsaken,
  nor his seed begging bread.
²⁶ He is ever merciful, and lendeth;
 and his seed is blessed.
²⁷ Depart from evil, and do good;
 and dwell for evermore.
²⁸ For the Lord loveth judgment,

and forsaketh not his saints;
>they are preserved for ever;
>but the seed of the wicked shall be cut off.
29 The righteous shall inherit the land,
>and dwell therein for ever.
30 The mouth of the righteous speaketh wisdom,
>and his tongue talketh of judgment.
31 The law of his God is in his heart;
>none of his steps shall slide.
32 The wicked watcheth the righteous,
>and seeketh to slay him.
33 The Lord will not leave him in his hand,
>nor condemn him when he is judged.
34 Wait on the Lord, and keep his way,
>and he shall exalt thee to inherit the land:
>>when the wicked are cut off,
>thou shalt see it.
35 I have seen the wicked in great power,
>and spreading himself like a green bay tree.
36 Yet he passed away, and, lo, he was not:
>yea, I sought him, but he could not be found.
37 Mark the perfect man, and behold the upright;
>for the end of that man is peace.
38 But the transgressors shall be destroyed together:
>the end of the wicked shall be cut off.
39 But the salvation of the righteous is of the Lord:
>he is their strength in the time of trouble.
40 And the Lord shall help them, and deliver them:

he shall deliver them from the wicked, and save
them, because they trust in him.

40

To the chief musician, a psalm of David.

I waited patiently for the Lord;
  and he inclined unto me, and heard my cry.
2 He brought me up also out of an horrible pit,
  out of the miry clay,
    and set my feet upon a rock,
  and established my goings.
3 And he hath put a new song in my mouth,
  even praise unto our God:
    many shall see it, and fear,
  and shall trust in the Lord.
4 Blessed is that man that maketh the Lord his trust,
  and respecteth not the proud,
    nor such as turn aside to lies.
5 Many, O Lord my God, are thy wonderful works
  which thou hast done,
    and thy thoughts which are to us-ward:
  they cannot be reckoned up in order unto thee:
    if I would declare and speak of them,
  they are more than can be numbered.
6 Sacrifice and offering thou didst not desire;
  mine ears hast thou opened:
    burnt offering and sin offering
  hast thou not required.

7 Then said I, 'Lo, I come:
  in the volume of the book it is written of me,
8 I delight to do thy will, O my God:
  yea, thy law is within my heart.'
9 I have preached righteousness in the great
    congregation: lo, I have not refrained my lips,
      O Lord, thou knowest.
10 I have not hid thy righteousness within my heart;
    I have declared thy faithfulness
      and thy salvation;
    I have not concealed thy lovingkindness
      and thy truth from the great congregation.
11 Withhold not thou thy tender mercies from me,
    O Lord: let thy lovingkindness
      and thy truth continually preserve me.
12 For innumerable evils have compassed me about:
    mine iniquities have taken hold upon me,
      so that I am not able to look up;
    they are more than the hairs of mine head;
      therefore my heart faileth me.
13 Be pleased, O Lord, to deliver me:
    O Lord, make haste to help me.
14 Let them be ashamed and confounded together
    that seek after my soul to destroy it;
      let them be driven backward
    and put to shame that wish me evil.
15 Let them be desolate for a reward of their shame
    that say unto me, 'Aha, aha.'

[16] Let all those that seek thee rejoice
and be glad in thee:
let such as love thy salvation say continually,
'The Lord be magnified.'
[17] But I am poor and needy;
yet the Lord thinketh upon me:
thou art my help and my deliverer;
make no tarrying, O my God.

42 To the chief musician, Maschil, for the sons
of Korah.

As the hart panteth after the water brooks,
so panteth my soul after thee, O God.
[2] My soul thirsteth for God, for the living God:
when shall I come and appear before God?
[3] My tears have been my meat day and night,
while they continually say unto me,
'Where is thy God?'
[4] When I remember these things,
I pour out my soul in me;
for I had gone with the multitude,
I went with them to the house of God,
with the voice of joy and praise,
with a multitude that kept holyday.
[5] Why art thou cast down, O my soul?
And why art thou disquieted in me?
Hope thou in God;

for I shall yet praise him for the help of his
    countenance.
⁶ O my God, my soul is cast down within me;
    therefore will I remember thee
        from the land of Jordan,
    and of the Hermonites, from the hill Mizar.
⁷ Deep calleth unto deep at the noise
    of thy waterspouts: all thy waves and thy billows
        are gone over me.
⁸ Yet the Lord will command his lovingkindness
    in the daytime,
        and in the night his song shall be with me,
    and my prayer unto the God of my life.
⁹ I will say unto God my rock,
    'Why hast thou forgotten me?
        Why go I mourning because of
    the oppression of the enemy?'
¹⁰ As with a sword in my bones,
    mine enemies reproach me;
        while they say daily unto me,
    'Where is thy God?'
¹¹ Why art thou cast down, O my soul?
    And why art thou disquieted within me?
        Hope thou in God;
    for I shall yet praise him, who is the health
    of my countenance, and my God.

46

To the chief musician for the sons of Korah,
a song upon Alamoth.

God is our refuge and strength,
a very present help in trouble.
2 Therefore will not we fear,
though the earth be removed,
and though the mountains be carried
into the midst of the sea;
3 though the waters thereof roar and be troubled,
though the mountains shake
with the swelling thereof. Selah.
4 There is a river, the streams whereof
shall make glad the city of God, the holy place
of the tabernacles of the most High.
5 God is in the midst of her;
she shall not be moved:
God shall help her, and that right early.
6 The heathen raged, the kingdoms were moved:
he uttered his voice, the earth melted.
7 The Lord of hosts is with us;
the God of Jacob is our refuge. Selah.
8 Come, behold the works of the Lord,
what desolations he hath made in the earth.
9 He maketh wars to cease unto the end of the earth;
he breaketh the bow,
and cutteth the spear in sunder;
he burneth the chariot in the fire.

¹⁰ Be still, and know that I am God:
    I will be exalted among the heathen,
        I will be exalted in the earth.
¹¹ The Lord of hosts is with us;
    the God of Jacob is our refuge. Selah.

47

To the chief Musician, a psalm for
the sons of Korah.

O clap your hands, all ye people;
    shout unto God with the voice of triumph.
² For the Lord most high is terrible;
    he is a great King over all the earth.
³ He shall subdue the people under us,
    and the nations under our feet.
⁴ He shall choose our inheritance for us,
    the excellency of Jacob whom he loved. Selah.
⁵ God is gone up with a shout,
    the Lord with the sound of a trumpet.
⁶ Sing praises to God, sing praises:
    sing praises unto our King, sing praises.
⁷ For God is the King of all the earth:
    sing ye praises with understanding.
⁸ God reigneth over the heathen:
    God sitteth upon the throne of his holiness.
⁹ The princes of the people are gathered together,
    even the people of the God of Abraham:
        for the shields of the earth belong unto God:

he is greatly exalted.

51
To the chief musician, a psalm of David,
when Nathan the prophet came unto him,
after he had gone in to Bath-sheba.

Have mercy upon me, O God,
according to thy lovingkindness:
according unto the multitude
of thy tender mercies blot out my transgressions.
² Wash me throughly from mine iniquity,
and cleanse me from my sin.
³ For I acknowledge my transgressions:
and my sin is ever before me.
⁴Against thee, thee only, have I sinned,
and done this evil in thy sight:
that thou mightest be justified
when thou speakest,
and be clear when thou judgest.
⁵ Behold, I was shapen in iniquity;
and in sin did my mother conceive me.
⁶ Behold, thou desirest truth in the inward parts;
and in the hidden part thou shalt make me
to know wisdom.
⁷ Purge me with hyssop, and I shall be clean:
wash me, and I shall be whiter than snow.
⁸ Make me to hear joy and gladness;
that the bones which thou hast broken

                    may rejoice.
⁹ Hide thy face from my sins,
        and blot out all mine iniquities.
¹⁰ Create in me a clean heart, O God;
        and renew a right spirit within me.
¹¹ Cast me not away from thy presence;
        and take not thy holy spirit from me.
¹² Restore unto me the joy of thy salvation;
        and uphold me with thy free spirit.
¹³ Then will I teach transgressors thy ways;
        and sinners shall be converted unto thee.
¹⁴ Deliver me from bloodguiltiness, O God,
        thou God of my salvation;
            and my tongue shall sing aloud
        of thy righteousness.
¹⁵ O Lord, open thou my lips;
        and my mouth shall shew forth thy praise.
¹⁶ For thou desirest not sacrifice;
        else would I give it:
            thou delightest not in burnt offering.
¹⁷ The sacrifices of God are a broken spirit:
        a broken and a contrite heart, O God,
            thou wilt not despise.
¹⁸ Do good in thy good pleasure unto Zion:
        build thou the walls of Jerusalem.
¹⁹ Then shalt thou be pleased with the sacrifices
        of righteousness,
            with burnt offering and whole burnt offering:

then shall they offer bullocks upon thine altar.

55

To the chief musician on Neginoth, Maschil, a psalm of David.

Give ear to my prayer, O God;
  and hide not thyself from my supplication.
²Attend unto me, and hear me:
  I mourn in my complaint, and make a noise;
³ because of the voice of the enemy,
    because of the oppression of the wicked;
      for they cast iniquity upon me,
      and in wrath they hate me.
⁴My heart is sore pained within me;
  and the terrors of death are fallen upon me.
⁵Fearfulness and trembling are come upon me,
  and horror hath overwhelmed me.
⁶And I said, 'Oh that I had wings like a dove!
  For then would I fly away, and be at rest.
⁷Lo, then would I wander far off,
  and remain in the wilderness. Selah.
⁸I would hasten my escape from the windy storm
  and tempest.'
⁹Destroy, O Lord, and divide their tongues;
  for I have seen violence and strife in the city.
¹⁰Day and night they go about it
    upon the walls thereof: mischief also and sorrow
      are in the midst of it.

[11] Wickedness is in the midst thereof:
 deceit and guile depart not from her streets.
[12] For it was not an enemy that reproached me;
 then I could have borne it:
  neither was it he that hated me that did
 magnify himself against me;
  then I would have hid myself from him.
[13] But it was thou, a man mine equal,
 my guide, and mine acquaintance.
[14] We took sweet counsel together, and walked
 unto the house of God in company.
[15] Let death seize upon them,
 and let them go down quick into hell;
  for wickedness is in their dwellings,
 and among them.
[16] As for me, I will call upon God;
 and the Lord shall save me.
[17] Evening, and morning, and at noon,
 will I pray, and cry aloud;
  and he shall hear my voice.
[18] He hath delivered my soul in peace
 from the battle that was against me;
  for there were many with me.
[19] God shall hear, and afflict them,
 even he that abideth of old. Selah.
  Because they have no changes,
 therefore they fear not God.
[20] He hath put forth his hands against such as

be at peace with him:
>> he hath broken his covenant.
²¹ The words of his mouth were smoother than butter,
>> but war was in his heart:
>>> his words were softer than oil,
>> yet were they drawn swords.
²² Cast thy burden upon the Lord,
>> and he shall sustain thee: he shall
>>> never suffer the righteous to be moved.
²³ But thou, O God, shalt bring them down
>> into the pit of destruction:
>>> bloody and deceitful men shall not live out
>> half their days; but I will trust in thee.

56 To the chief musician upon Jonath-elem-rechokim,
Michtam of David, when the Philistines
took him in Gath.

Be merciful unto me, O God;
>> for man would swallow me up;
>>> he fighting daily oppresseth me.
² Mine enemies would daily swallow me up;
>> for they be many that fight against me,
>>> O thou most High.
³ What time I am afraid, I will trust in thee.
⁴ In God I will praise his word,
>> in God I have put my trust;
>>> I will not fear what flesh can do unto me.

⁵ Every day they wrest my words:
    all their thoughts are against me for evil.
⁶ They gather themselves together,
    they hide themselves, they mark my steps,
        when they wait for my soul.
⁷ Shall they escape by iniquity?
    In thine anger cast down the people, O God.
⁸ Thou tellest my wanderings:
    put thou my tears into thy bottle:
        are they not in thy book?
⁹ When I cry unto thee,
        then shall mine enemies turn back:
    this I know; for God is for me.
¹⁰ In God will I praise his word:
    in the Lord will I praise his word.
¹¹ In God have I put my trust:
    I will not be afraid what man can do unto me.
¹² Thy vows are upon me, O God:
    I will render praises unto thee.
¹³ For thou hast delivered my soul from death:
    wilt not thou deliver my feet from falling,
        that I may walk before God
    in the light of the living?

62

To the chief musician, to Jeduthun,
    a psalm of David.

Truly my soul waiteth upon God:

from him cometh my salvation.

² He only is my rock and my salvation;
he is my defence; I shall not be greatly moved.

³ How long will ye imagine mischief against a man?
Ye shall be slain all of you:
as a bowing wall shall ye be,
and as a tottering fence.

⁴ They only consult to cast him down
from his excellency: they delight in lies:
they bless with their mouth,
but they curse inwardly. Selah.

⁵ My soul, wait thou only upon God;
for my expectation is from him.

⁶ He only is my rock and my salvation;
he is my defence; I shall not be moved.

⁷ In God is my salvation and my glory:
the rock of my strength,
and my refuge, is in God.

⁸ Trust in him at all times;
ye people, pour out your heart before him:
God is a refuge for us. Selah.

⁹ Surely men of low degree are vanity,
and men of high degree are a lie:
to be laid in the balance,
they are altogether lighter than vanity.

¹⁰ Trust not in oppression,
and become not vain in robbery:
if riches increase, set not your heart upon them.

¹¹God hath spoken once; twice have I heard this;
  that power belongeth unto God.
¹²Also unto thee, O Lord, belongeth mercy:
  for thou renderest to every man
  according to his work.

63 A psalm of David, when he was in the wilderness
  of Judah.

O God, thou art my God; early will I seek thee:
  my soul thirsteth for thee,
    my flesh longeth for thee in a dry and thirsty
  land,
    where no water is,
² to see thy power and thy glory,
  so as I have seen thee in the sanctuary.
³ Because thy lovingkindness is better than life,
  my lips shall praise thee.
⁴ Thus will I bless thee while I live:
  I will lift up my hands in thy name.
⁵ My soul shall be satisfied as with marrow
  and fatness; and my mouth shall praise thee
    with joyful lips:
⁶ when I remember thee upon my bed,
  and meditate on thee in the night watches.
⁷ Because thou hast been my help,
  therefore in the shadow of thy wings
    will I rejoice.

⁸ My soul followeth hard after thee:
>   thy right hand upholdeth me.
⁹ But those that seek my soul, to destroy it,
>   shall go into the lower parts of the earth.
¹⁰ They shall fall by the sword:
>   they shall be a portion for foxes.
¹¹ But the king shall rejoice in God;
>   every one that sweareth by him shall glory:
>> but the mouth of them that speak lies
>   shall be stopped.

65

To the chief musician, a psalm and song of David.

Praise waiteth for thee, O God, in Sion:
>   and unto thee shall the vow be performed.
² O thou that hearest prayer,
>   unto thee shall all flesh come.
³ Iniquities prevail against me:
>   as for our transgressions,
>> thou shalt purge them away.
⁴ Blessed is the man whom thou choosest,
>   and causest to approach unto thee,
>> that he may dwell in thy courts:
>   we shall be satisfied with the goodness
>> of thy house, even of thy holy temple.
⁵ By terrible things in righteousness
>   wilt thou answer us,
>> O God of our salvation;

who art the confidence of all the ends
of the earth,
and of them that are afar off upon the sea;

⁶ Which by his strength setteth fast the mountains;
being girded with power;

⁷ Which stilleth the noise of the seas,
the noise of their waves,
and the tumult of the people.

⁸ They also that dwell in the uttermost parts
are afraid at thy tokens:
thou makest the outgoings of the morning
and evening to rejoice.

⁹ Thou visitest the earth, and waterest it:
thou greatly enrichest it with the river of God,
which is full of water:
thou preparest them corn,
when thou hast so provided for it.

¹⁰ Thou waterest the ridges thereof abundantly:
thou settlest the furrows thereof:
thou makest it soft with showers:
thou blessest the springing thereof.

¹¹ Thou crownest the year with thy goodness;
and thy paths drop fatness.

¹² They drop upon the pastures of the wilderness:
and the little hills rejoice on every side.

¹³ The pastures are clothed with flocks;
the valleys also are covered over with corn;
they shout for joy, they also sing.

66

To the chief musician, a song or psalm.

Make a joyful noise unto God, all ye lands:
² sing forth the honour of his name:
    make his praise glorious.
³ Say unto God,
        'How terrible art thou in thy works!
            Through the greatness of thy power
        shall thine enemies submit themselves unto thee.
⁴ All the earth shall worship thee,
        and shall sing unto thee;
            they shall sing to thy name.' Selah.
⁵ Come and see the works of God:
        he is terrible in his doing toward
            the children of men.
⁶ He turned the sea into dry land:
        they went through the flood on foot:
            there did we rejoice in him.
⁷ He ruleth by his power for ever;
        his eyes behold the nations: let not
            the rebellious exalt themselves. Selah.
⁸ O bless our God, ye people,
        and make the voice of his praise to be heard,
⁹ Which holdeth our soul in life,
        and suffereth not our feet to be moved.
¹⁰ For thou, O God, hast proved us:
        thou hast tried us, as silver is tried.
¹¹ Thou broughtest us into the net;

thou laidst affliction upon our loins.

¹² Thou hast caused men to ride over our heads;
we went through fire and through water:
but thou broughtest us out
into a wealthy place.

¹³ I will go into thy house with burnt offerings:
I will pay thee my vows,

¹⁴ which my lips have uttered, and my mouth hath
spoken, when I was in trouble.

¹⁵ I will offer unto thee burnt sacrifices of fatlings,
with the incense of rams;
I will offer bullocks with goats. Selah.

¹⁶ Come and hear, all ye that fear God,
and I will declare what he hath done
for my soul.

¹⁷ I cried unto him with my mouth,
and he was extolled with my tongue.

¹⁸ If I regard iniquity in my heart,
the Lord will not hear me:

¹⁹ but verily God hath heard me;
he hath attended to the voice of my prayer.

²⁰ Blessed be God, which hath not turned away
my prayer, nor his mercy from me.

67

To the chief musician on Neginoth, a psalm or song.

God be merciful unto us, and bless us;
and cause his face to shine upon us; Selah.

² That thy way may be known upon earth,
    thy saving health among all nations.
³ Let the people praise thee, O God;
    let all the people praise thee.
⁴ O let the nations be glad and sing for joy:
    for thou shalt judge the people righteously,
        and govern the nations upon earth. Selah.
⁵ Let the people praise thee, O God;
    let all the people praise thee.
⁶ Then shall the earth yield her increase;
    and God, even our own God, shall bless us.
⁷ God shall bless us; and all the ends of the earth
    shall fear him.

72

A psalm for Solomon.

Give the king thy judgments, O God,
    and thy righteousness unto the king's son.
² He shall judge thy people with righteousness,
    and thy poor with judgment.
³ The mountains shall bring peace to the people,
    and the little hills, by righteousness.
⁴ He shall judge the poor of the people,
    he shall save the children of the needy,
        and shall break in pieces the oppressor.
⁵ They shall fear thee as long as the sun
    and moon endure, throughout all generations.
⁶ He shall come down like rain upon the mown grass,

as showers that water the earth.
⁷ In his days shall the righteous flourish;
     and abundance of peace
          so long as the moon endureth.
⁸ He shall have dominion also from sea to sea,
     and from the river unto the ends of the earth.
⁹ They that dwell in the wilderness shall bow
     before him;
          and his enemies shall lick the dust.
¹⁰ The kings of Tarshish and of the isles
     shall bring presents:
          the kings of Sheba and Seba shall offer gifts.
¹¹ Yea, all kings shall fall down before him:
     all nations shall serve him.
¹² For he shall deliver the needy when he crieth;
     the poor also, and him that hath no helper.
¹³ He shall spare the poor and needy,
     and shall save the souls of the needy.
¹⁴ He shall redeem their soul from deceit
     and violence: and precious
          shall their blood be in his sight.
¹⁵ And he shall live, and to him shall be given
     of the gold of Sheba:
          prayer also shall be made for him continu-
     ally;
          and daily shall he be praised.
¹⁶ There shall be an handful of corn in the earth
     upon the top of the mountains;

the fruit thereof shall shake like Lebanon:
and they of the city shall flourish
like grass of the earth.
¹⁷ His name shall endure for ever:
his name shall be continued as long as the sun:
and men shall be blessed in him:
all nations shall call him blessed.
¹⁸ Blessed be the Lord God, the God of Israel,
who only doeth wondrous things.
¹⁹ And blessed be his glorious name for ever:
and let the whole earth be filled with his glory;
Amen, and Amen.
²⁰ The prayers of David the son of Jesse are ended.

80

To the chief musician upon Shoshannim-Eduth,
a psalm of Asaph.

Give ear, O Shepherd of Israel,
thou that leadest Joseph like a flock;
thou that dwellest between the cherubims,
shine forth.
² Before Ephraim and Benjamin and Manasseh
stir up thy strength, and come and save us.
³ Turn us again, O God, and cause thy face to shine;
and we shall be saved.
⁴ O Lord God of hosts, how long wilt thou be angry
against the prayer of thy people.
⁵ Thou feedest them with the bread of tears;

and givest them tears to drink in great measure.
⁶ Thou makest us a strife unto our neighbours;
and our enemies laugh among themselves.
⁷ Turn us again, O God of hosts,
and cause thy face to shine; and we shall be saved.
⁸ Thou hast brought a vine out of Egypt:
thou hast cast out the heathen, and planted it.
⁹ Thou preparedst room before it,
and didst cause it to take deep root,
and it filled the land.
¹⁰ The hills were covered with the shadow of it,
and the boughs thereof were
like the goodly cedars.
¹¹ She sent out her boughs unto the sea,
and her branches unto the river.
¹² Why hast thou then broken down her hedges,
so that all they which pass by the way
do pluck her?
¹³ The boar out of the wood doth waste it,
and the wild beast of the field doth devour it.
¹⁴ Return, we beseech thee, O God of hosts:
look down from heaven, and behold,
and visit this vine;
¹⁵ and the vineyard which thy right hand
hath planted, and the branch
that thou madest strong for thyself.
¹⁶ It is burned with fire, it is cut down:
they perish at the rebuke of thy countenance.
¹⁷ Let thy hand be upon the man of thy right hand,

upon the son of man
>> whom thou madest strong for thyself.
¹⁸ So will not we go back from thee:
>> quicken us, and we will call upon thy name.
¹⁹ Turn us again, O Lord God of hosts,
>> cause thy face to shine;
>>> and we shall be saved.

84

To the chief musician upon Gittith, a psalm for the sons of Korah.

How amiable are thy tabernacles, O Lord of hosts!
² My soul longeth, yea, even fainteth
>> for the courts of the Lord:
>>> my heart and my flesh crieth out
>>> for the living God.
³ Yea, the sparrow hath found an house,
>> and the swallow a nest for herself,
>>> where she may lay her young,
>> even thine altars, O Lord of hosts,
>>> my King, and my God.
⁴ Blessed are they that dwell in thy house:
>> they will be still praising thee. Selah.
⁵ Blessed is the man whose strength is in thee:
>> in whose heart are the ways of them.
⁶ Who passing through the valley of Baca
>> make it a well;
>>> the rain also filleth the pools.

⁷ They go from strength to strength,
   every one of them in Zion appeareth before God.
⁸ O Lord God of hosts, hear my prayer:
   give ear, O God of Jacob. Selah.
⁹ Behold, O God our shield,
   and look upon the face of thine anointed.
¹⁰ For a day in thy courts is better than a thousand.
   I had rather be a doorkeeper
      in the house of my God,
   than to dwell in the tents of wickedness.
¹¹ For the Lord God is a sun and shield:
   the Lord will give grace and glory:
      no good thing will he withhold
   from them that walk uprightly.
¹² O Lord of hosts,
   blessed is the man that trusteth in thee.

87

A psalm or song for the sons of Korah.

His foundation is in the holy mountains.
² The Lord loveth the gates of Zion
   more than all the dwellings of Jacob.
³ Glorious things are spoken of thee,
   O city of God. Selah.
⁴ I will make mention of Rahab and Babylon
   to them that know me: behold Philistia,
      and Tyre, with Ethiopia; this man was born
   there.

⁵And of Zion it shall be said,
  'This and that man was born in her':
    and the highest himself shall establish her.
⁶ The Lord shall count,
  when he writeth up the people,
    that this man was born there. Selah.
⁷As well the singers as the players on instruments
  shall be there: all my springs are in thee.

89

Maschil of Ethan the Ezrahite.

I will sing of the mercies of the Lord for ever:
  with my mouth will I make known
thy faithfulness to all generations.
² For I have said, 'Mercy shall be built up for ever:
  thy faithfulness shalt thou establish
    in the very heavens.'
³ I have made a covenant with my chosen,
  I have sworn unto David my servant,
⁴ 'Thy seed will I establish for ever,
  and build up thy throne to all generations.' Selah.
⁵And the heavens shall praise thy wonders, O Lord:
  thy faithfulness also in the congregation
    of the saints.
⁶ For who in the heaven can be compared
  unto the Lord?
    Who among the sons of the mighty
    can be likened unto the Lord?

⁷God is greatly to be feared in the assembly
of the saints, and to be had in reverence
of all them that are about him.
⁸O Lord God of hosts, who is a strong Lord
like unto thee?
Or to thy faithfulness round about thee?
⁹Thou rulest the raging of the sea:
when the waves thereof arise, thou stillest them.
¹⁰Thou hast broken Rahab in pieces,
as one that is slain;
thou hast scattered thine enemies
with thy strong arm.
¹¹The heavens are thine, the earth also is thine:
as for the world and the fulness thereof,
thou hast founded them.
¹²The north and the south thou hast created them:
Tabor and Hermon shall rejoice in thy name.
¹³Thou hast a mighty arm:
strong is thy hand, and high is thy right hand.
¹⁴Justice and judgment are the habitation
of thy throne:
mercy and truth shall go before thy face.
¹⁵Blessed is the people that know the joyful sound:
they shall walk, O Lord,
in the light of thy countenance.
¹⁶In thy name shall they rejoice all the day;
and in thy righteousness shall they be exalted.
¹⁷For thou art the glory of their strength;

and in thy favour our horn shall be exalted.

¹⁸ For the Lord is our defence;
and the Holy One of Israel is our king.
¹⁹ Then thou spakest in vision to thy holy one,
and saidst,
'I have laid help upon one that is mighty;
I have exalted one chosen out of the people.
²⁰ I have found David my servant;
with my holy oil have I anointed him,
²¹ with whom my hand shall be established:
mine arm also shall strengthen him.
²² The enemy shall not exact upon him;
nor the son of wickedness afflict him.
²³ And I will beat down his foes before his face,
and plague them that hate him.
²⁴ But my faithfulness and my mercy
shall be with him;
and in my name shall his horn be exalted.
²⁵ I will set his hand also in the sea,
and his right hand in the rivers.
²⁶ He shall cry unto me,
"Thou art my father, my God,
and the rock of my salvation."
²⁷ Also I will make him my firstborn,
higher than the kings of the earth.
²⁸ My mercy will I keep for him for evermore,
and my covenant shall stand fast with him.
²⁹ His seed also will I make to endure for ever,

and his throne as the days of heaven.
³⁰ If his children forsake my law,
and walk not in my judgments;
³¹ if they break my statutes,
and keep not my commandments;
³² then will I visit their transgression with the rod,
and their iniquity with stripes.
³³ Nevertheless my lovingkindness will I not
utterly take from him,
nor suffer my faithfulness to fail.
³⁴ My covenant will I not break,
nor alter the thing that is gone out of my lips.
³⁵ Once have I sworn by my holiness
that I will not lie unto David.
³⁶ His seed shall endure for ever,
and his throne as the sun before me.
³⁷ It shall be established for ever as the moon,
and as a faithful witness in heaven.' Selah.
³⁸ But thou hast cast off and abhorred,
thou hast been wroth with thine anointed.
³⁹ Thou hast made void the covenant of thy servant:
thou hast profaned his crown
by casting it to the ground.
⁴⁰ Thou hast broken down all his hedges;
thou hast brought his strong holds to ruin.
⁴¹ All that pass by the way spoil him:
he is a reproach to his neighbours.
⁴² Thou hast set up the right hand of his adversaries;

thou hast made all his enemies to rejoice.
⁴³ Thou hast also turned the edge of his sword,
and hast not made him to stand in the battle.
⁴⁴ Thou hast made his glory to cease,
and cast his throne down to the ground.
⁴⁵ The days of his youth hast thou shortened:
thou hast covered him with shame. Selah.
⁴⁶ How long, Lord?
Wilt thou hide thyself for ever?
Shall thy wrath burn like fire?
⁴⁷ Remember how short my time is:
wherefore hast thou made all men in vain?
⁴⁸ What man is he that liveth, and shall not see death?
Shall he deliver his soul from the hand
of the grave? Selah.
⁴⁹ Lord, where are thy former lovingkindnesses,
which thou swarest unto David in thy truth?
⁵⁰ Remember, Lord, the reproach of thy servants;
how I do bear in my bosom the reproach
of all the mighty people;
⁵¹ wherewith thine enemies have reproached, O Lord;
wherewith they have reproached the footsteps
of thine anointed.
⁵² Blessed be the Lord for evermore.
Amen, and Amen.

90

A prayer of Moses the man of God.

Lord, thou hast been our dwelling place
     in all generations.
[2] Before the mountains were brought forth,
     or ever thou hadst formed the earth
          and the world,
     even from everlasting
          to everlasting, thou art God.
[3] Thou turnest man to destruction; and sayest,
     'Return, ye children of men.'
[4] For a thousand years in thy sight
     are but as yesterday when it is past,
          and as a watch in the night.
[5] Thou carriest them away as with a flood;
     they are as a sleep: in the morning they are like grass
     which groweth up.
[6] In the morning it flourisheth, and groweth up;
     in the evening it is cut down, and withereth.
[7] For we are consumed by thine anger,
     and by thy wrath are we troubled.
[8] Thou hast set our iniquities before thee,
     our secret sins in the light of thy countenance.
[9] For all our days are passed away in thy wrath:
     we spend our years as a tale that is told.
[10] The days of our years are three-score years and ten;
     and if by reason of strength
          they be fourscore years,

yet is their strength labour and sorrow;
    for it is soon cut off, and we fly away.
¹¹ Who knoweth the power of thine anger?
    Even according to thy fear, so is thy wrath.
¹² So teach us to number our days,
    that we may apply our hearts unto wisdom.
¹³ Return, O Lord, how long?
    And let it repent thee concerning thy servants.
¹⁴ O satisfy us early with thy mercy;
    that we may rejoice and be glad all our days.
¹⁵ Make us glad according to the days
    wherein thou hast afflicted us,
        and the years wherein we have seen evil.
¹⁶ Let thy work appear unto thy servants,
    and thy glory unto their children.
¹⁷ And let the beauty of the Lord our God be upon us;
    and establish thou the work of our hands upon us;
    yea, the work of our hands establish thou it.

91 He that dwelleth in the secret place of the most High
    shall abide under the shadow of the Almighty.
² I will say of the Lord,
    'He is my refuge and my fortress:
        my God; in him will I trust.'
³ Surely he shall deliver thee from the snare
    of the fowler,
        and from the noisome pestilence.

⁴He shall cover thee with his feathers,
　　and under his wings shalt thou trust:
　　　　his truth shall be thy shield and buckler.
⁵Thou shalt not be afraid for the terror by night;
　　nor for the arrow that flieth by day;
⁶nor for the pestilence that walketh in darkness;
　　nor for the destruction that wasteth at noonday.
⁷A thousand shall fall at thy side,
　　and ten thousand at thy right hand;
　　　　but it shall not come nigh thee.
⁸Only with thine eyes shalt thou behold
　　and see the reward of the wicked.
⁹Because thou hast made the Lord,
　　which is my refuge,
　　　　even the most High, thy habitation;
¹⁰there shall no evil befall thee,
　　neither shall any plague come nigh thy dwelling.
¹¹For he shall give his angels charge over thee,
　　to keep thee in all thy ways.
¹²They shall bear thee up in their hands,
　　lest thou dash thy foot against a stone.
¹³Thou shalt tread upon the lion and adder:
　　the young lion and the dragon
　　　　shalt thou trample under feet.
¹⁴Because he hath set his love upon me,
　　therefore will I deliver him:
　　　　I will set him on high,
　　because he hath known my name.

¹⁵ He shall call upon me,
>   and I will answer him;
>   I will be with him in trouble;
>   I will deliver him, and honour him.
¹⁶ With long life will I satisfy him,
>   and shew him my salvation.

92

A psalm or song for the sabbath day.

> It is a good thing to give thanks unto the Lord,
>   and to sing praises unto thy name,
> O most High,
² to shew forth thy lovingkindness in the morning,
>   and thy faithfulness every night,
³ upon an instrument of ten strings,
>   and upon the psaltery;
>   upon the harp with a solemn sound.
⁴ For thou, Lord, hast made me glad
>   through thy work:
>   I will triumph in the works of thy hands.
⁵ O Lord, how great are thy works!
>   And thy thoughts are very deep.
⁶ A brutish man knoweth not;
>   neither doth a fool understand this.
⁷ When the wicked spring as the grass,
>   and when all the workers of iniquity do flourish;
>   it is that they shall be destroyed for ever;
⁸ but thou, Lord, art most high for evermore.

⁹ For, lo, thine enemies, O Lord,
    for, lo, thine enemies shall perish;
        all the workers of iniquity shall be scattered.
¹⁰ But my horn shalt thou exalt like the horn
    of an unicorn:
        I shall be anointed with fresh oil.
¹¹ Mine eye also shall see my desire on mine enemies,
    and mine ears shall hear my desire
        of the wicked that rise up against me.
¹² The righteous shall flourish like the palm tree:
    he shall grow like a cedar in Lebanon.
¹³ Those that be planted in the house of the Lord
    shall flourish in the courts of our God.
¹⁴ They shall still bring forth fruit in old age;
    they shall be fat and flourishing;
¹⁵ to shew that the Lord is upright: he is my rock,
    and there is no unrighteousness in him.

93 The Lord reigneth, he is clothed with majesty;
    the Lord is clothed with strength,
    wherewith he hath girded himself:
    the world also is stablished,
    that it cannot be moved.
² Thy throne is established of old:
    thou art from everlasting.
³ The floods have lifted up, O Lord,
    the floods have lifted up their voice;

the floods lift up their waves.
⁴ The Lord on high is mightier than the noise
of many waters,
yea, than the mighty waves of the sea.
⁵ Thy testimonies are very sure:
holiness becometh thine house, O Lord, for ever.

95

O come, let us sing unto the Lord:
let us make a joyful noise to the rock
of our salvation.
² Let us come before his presence with thanksgiving,
and make a joyful noise unto him with psalms.
³ For the Lord is a great God,
and a great King above all gods.
⁴ In his hand are the deep places of the earth:
the strength of the hills is his also.
⁵ The sea is his, and he made it;
and his hands formed the dry land.
⁶ O come, let us worship and bow down:
let us kneel before the Lord our maker.
⁷ For he is our God;
and we are the people of his pasture,
and the sheep of his hand.
To day if ye will hear his voice,
⁸ harden not your heart, as in the provocation,
and as in the day of temptation in the wilderness;
⁹ when your fathers tempted me,

proved me, and saw my work.

¹⁰ Forty years long was I grieved with this generation,
    and said, 'It is a people that do err in their heart,
        and they have not known my ways,'

¹¹ unto whom I sware in my wrath that they should
    not enter into my rest.

96

O sing unto the Lord a new song:
    sing unto the Lord, all the earth.

² Sing unto the Lord, bless his name;
    shew forth his salvation from day to day.

³ Declare his glory among the heathen,
    his wonders among all people.

⁴ For the Lord is great, and greatly to be praised:
    he is to be feared above all gods.

⁵ For all the gods of the nations are idols;
    but the Lord made the heavens.

⁶ Honour and majesty are before him:
    strength and beauty are in his sanctuary.

⁷ Give unto the Lord, O ye kindreds of the people,
    give unto the Lord glory and strength.

⁸ Give unto the Lord the glory due unto his name:
    bring an offering, and come into his courts.

⁹ O worship the Lord in the beauty of holiness:
    fear before him, all the earth.

¹⁰ Say among the heathen that the Lord reigneth:
    the world also shall be established

that it shall not be moved:
he shall judge the people righteously.
¹¹ Let the heavens rejoice, and let the earth be glad;
let the sea roar, and the fulness thereof.
¹² Let the field be joyful, and all that is therein;
then shall all the trees of the wood rejoice
¹³ before the Lord; for he cometh,
for he cometh to judge the earth:
he shall judge the world with righteousness,
and the people with his truth.

97 The Lord reigneth; let the earth rejoice;
let the multitude of isles be glad thereof.
² Clouds and darkness are round about him:
righteousness and judgment are the habitation
of his throne.
³ A fire goeth before him,
and burneth up his enemies round about.
⁴ His lightnings enlightened the world:
the earth saw, and trembled.
⁵ The hills melted like wax at the presence
of the Lord,
at the presence of the Lord of the whole earth.
⁶ The heavens declare his righteousness,
and all the people see his glory.
⁷ Confounded be all they that serve graven images,
that boast themselves of idols:

worship him, all ye gods.
⁸ Zion heard, and was glad;
    and the daughters of Judah rejoiced
        because of thy judgments, O Lord.
⁹ For thou, Lord, art high above all the earth:
    thou art exalted far above all gods.
¹⁰ Ye that love the Lord, hate evil;
    he preserveth the souls of his saints;
        he delivereth them out of the hand
    of the wicked.
¹¹ Light is sown for the righteous,
    and gladness for the upright in heart.
¹² Rejoice in the Lord, ye righteous;
    and give thanks at the remembrance
        of his holiness.

.

98 A psalm.

O sing unto the Lord a new song;
    for he hath done marvellous things:
his right hand, and his holy arm,
    hath gotten him the victory.
² The Lord hath made known his salvation:
    his righteousness hath he openly shewed
        in the sight of the heathen.
³ He hath remembered his mercy and his truth
    toward the house of Israel:
        all the ends of the earth have seen

the salvation of our God.
⁴ Make a joyful noise unto the Lord,
all the earth: make a loud noise,
and rejoice, and sing praise.
⁵ Sing unto the Lord with the harp;
with the harp, and the voice of a psalm.
⁶ With trumpets and sound of cornet
make a joyful noise before the Lord, the King.
⁷ Let the sea roar, and the fulness thereof;
the world, and they that dwell therein.
⁸ Let the floods clap their hands;
let the hills be joyful together
⁹ Before the Lord; for he cometh to judge the earth;
with righteousness shall he judge the world,
and the people with equity.

100 A Psalm of praise.

Make a joyful noise unto the Lord, all ye lands.
² Serve the Lord with gladness:
come before his presence with singing.
³ Know ye that the Lord he is God;
it is he that hath made us, and not we ourselves;
we are his people,
and the sheep of his pasture.
⁴ Enter into his gates with thanksgiving,
and into his courts with praise:
be thankful unto him, and bless his name.

⁵ For the Lord is good; his mercy is everlasting;
    and his truth endureth to all generations.

102 A prayer of the afflicted, when he is
overwhelmed, and poureth out his complaint
before the Lord.

Hear my prayer, O Lord,
    and let my cry come unto thee.
² Hide not thy face from me in the day
    when I am in trouble; incline thine ear unto me:
        in the day when I call answer me speedily.
³ For my days are consumed like smoke,
    and my bones are burned as an hearth.
⁴ My heart is smitten, and withered like grass;
    so that I forget to eat my bread.
⁵ By reason of the voice of my groaning my bones
    cleave to my skin.
⁶ I am like a pelican of the wilderness:
    I am like an owl of the desert.
⁷ I watch, and am as a sparrow
    alone upon the house top.
⁸ Mine enemies reproach me all the day;
    and they that are mad against me are sworn
        against me.
⁹ For I have eaten ashes like bread,
    and mingled my drink with weeping,
¹⁰ because of thine indignation and thy wrath;

for thou hast lifted me up, and cast me down.
¹¹ My days are like a shadow that declineth;
  and I am withered like grass.
¹² But thou, O Lord, shalt endure for ever;
  and thy remembrance unto all generations.
¹³ Thou shalt arise, and have mercy upon Zion;
  for the time to favour her, yea,
    the set time, is come.
¹⁴ For thy servants take pleasure in her stones,
  and favour the dust thereof.
¹⁵ So the heathen shall fear the name of the Lord,
  and all the kings of the earth thy glory.
¹⁶ When the Lord shall build up Zion,
  he shall appear in his glory.
¹⁷ He will regard the prayer of the destitute,
  and not despise their prayer.
¹⁸ This shall be written for the generation to come;
  and the people which shall be created
    shall praise the Lord.
¹⁹ For he hath looked down from the height
  of his sanctuary;
    from heaven did the Lord behold the earth;
²⁰ to hear the groaning of the prisoner;
  to loose those that are appointed to death;
²¹ to declare the name of the Lord in Zion,
  and his praise in Jerusalem;
²² when the people are gathered together,
  and the kingdoms, to serve the Lord.

²³ He weakened my strength in the way;
  he shortened my days.
²⁴ I said, 'O my God, take me not away
    in the midst of my days;
      thy years are throughout all generations.'
²⁵ Of old hast thou laid the foundation of the earth;
    and the heavens are the work of thy hands.
²⁶ They shall perish, but thou shalt endure:
    yea, all of them shall wax old like a garment;
      as a vesture shalt thou change them,
    and they shall be changed;
²⁷ but thou art the same,
    and thy years shall have no end.
²⁸ The children of thy servants shall continue,
    and their seed shall be established before thee.

103

A psalm of David.

Bless the Lord, O my soul;
      and all that is within me, bless his holy name.
² Bless the Lord, O my soul,
    and forget not all his benefits;
³ who forgiveth all thine iniquities;
    who healeth all thy diseases;
⁴ who redeemeth thy life from destruction;
    who crowneth thee with lovingkindness
      and tender mercies;
⁵ who satisfieth thy mouth with good things;

so that thy youth is renewed like the eagle's.
⁶ The Lord executeth righteousness
and judgment for all that are oppressed.
⁷ He made known his ways unto Moses,
his acts unto the children of Israel.
⁸ The Lord is merciful and gracious,
slow to anger, and plenteous in mercy.
⁹ He will not always chide;
neither will he keep his anger for ever.
¹⁰ He hath not dealt with us after our sins;
nor rewarded us according to our iniquities.
¹¹ For as the heaven is high above the earth,
so great is his mercy toward them that fear him.
¹² As far as the east is from the west,
so far hath he removed our transgressions
from us.
¹³ Like as a father pitieth his children,
so the Lord pitieth them that fear him.
¹⁴ For he knoweth our frame;
he remembereth that we are dust.
¹⁵ As for man, his days are as grass:
as a flower of the field, so he flourisheth.
¹⁶ For the wind passeth over it, and it is gone;
and the place thereof shall know it no more.
¹⁷ But the mercy of the Lord is from everlasting
to everlasting upon them that fear him,
and his righteousness unto children's children;
¹⁸ to such as keep his covenant,

and to those that remember his commandments
to do them.
¹⁹ The Lord hath prepared his throne in the heavens;
and his kingdom ruleth over all.
²⁰ Bless the Lord, ye his angels, that excel in strength,
that do his commandments,
hearkening unto the voice of his word.
²¹ Bless ye the Lord, all ye his hosts;
ye ministers of his, that do his pleasure.
²² Bless the Lord, all his works in all places
of his dominion: bless the Lord, O my soul.

104 Bless the Lord, O my soul.
O Lord my God, thou art very great;
thou art clothed with honour and majesty.
² Who coverest thyself with light as with a garment;
who stretchest out the heavens like a curtain;
³ who layeth the beams of his chambers
in the waters;
who maketh the clouds his chariot;
who walketh upon the wings of the wind;
⁴ who maketh his angels spirits;
his ministers a flaming fire;
⁵ who laid the foundations of the earth,
that it should not be removed for ever.
⁶ Thou coveredst it with the deep as with a garment:
the waters stood above the mountains.

⁷At thy rebuke they fled;
  at the voice of thy thunder they hasted away.
⁸ They go up by the mountains;
  they go down by the valleys unto the place
    which thou hast founded for them.
⁹ Thou hast set a bound that they may not pass over;
  that they turn not again to cover the earth.
¹⁰ He sendeth the springs into the valleys,
  which run among the hills.
¹¹ They give drink to every beast of the field:
  the wild asses quench their thirst.
¹² By them shall the fowls of the heaven
  have their habitation,
    which sing among the branches.
¹³ He watereth the hills from his chambers:
  the earth is satisfied with the fruit of thy works.
¹⁴ He causeth the grass to grow for the cattle,
  and herb for the service of man,
    that he may bring forth food out of the earth;
¹⁵ and wine that maketh glad the heart of man,
  and oil to make his face to shine,
    and bread which strengtheneth man's heart.
¹⁶ The trees of the Lord are full of sap;
  the cedars of Lebanon, which he hath planted;
¹⁷ where the birds make their nests:
  as for the stork, the fir trees are her house.
¹⁸ The high hills are a refuge for the wild goats;
  and the rocks for the conies.

¹⁹ He appointed the moon for seasons;
    the sun knoweth his going down.
²⁰ Thou makest darkness, and it is night;
    wherein all the beasts of the forest do creep forth.
²¹ The young lions roar after their prey,
    and seek their meat from God.
²² The sun ariseth, they gather themselves together,
    and lay them down in their dens.
²³ Man goeth forth unto his work and to his labour
    until the evening.
²⁴ O Lord, how manifold are thy works!
    In wisdom hast thou made them all;
        the earth is full of thy riches.
²⁵ So is this great and wide sea,
    wherein are things creeping innumerable,
        both small and great beasts.
²⁶ There go the ships;
    there is that leviathan,
        whom thou hast made to play therein.
²⁷ These wait all upon thee,
    that thou mayest give them their meat
        in due season.
²⁸ That thou givest them they gather:
    thou openest thine hand,
        they are filled with good.
²⁹ Thou hidest thy face, they are troubled:
    thou takest away their breath,
        they die, and return to their dust.

³⁰ Thou sendest forth thy spirit, they are created:
  and thou renewest the face of the earth.
³¹ The glory of the Lord shall endure for ever:
  the Lord shall rejoice in his works.
³² He looketh on the earth, and it trembleth:
  he toucheth the hills, and they smoke.
³³ I will sing unto the Lord as long as I live:
  I will sing praise to my God
    while I have my being.
³⁴ My meditation of him shall be sweet:
  I will be glad in the Lord.
³⁵ Let the sinners be consumed out of the earth,
  and let the wicked be no more.
    Bless thou the Lord, O my soul.
  Praise ye the Lord.

105

O give thanks unto the Lord;
  call upon his name;
    make known his deeds among the people.
² Sing unto him, sing psalms unto him;
  talk ye of all his wondrous works.
³ Glory ye in his holy name;
  let the heart of them rejoice that seek the Lord.
⁴ Seek the Lord, and his strength;
  seek his face evermore.
⁵ Remember his marvellous works that he hath done;
  his wonders, and the judgments of his mouth;

⁶ O ye seed of Abraham his servant,
   ye children of Jacob his chosen.
⁷ He is the Lord our God;
   his judgments are in all the earth.
⁸ He hath remembered his covenant for ever,
   the word which he commanded
      to a thousand generations.
⁹ Which covenant he made with Abraham,
   and his oath unto Isaac;
¹⁰ and confirmed the same unto Jacob for a law,
   and to Israel for an everlasting covenant,
¹¹ saying, 'Unto thee will I give the land of Canaan,
   the lot of your inheritance,'
¹² when they were but a few men in number;
   yea, very few, and strangers in it.
¹³ When they went from one nation to another,
   from one kingdom to another people;
¹⁴ he suffered no man to do them wrong:
   yea, he reproved kings for their sakes,
¹⁵ saying, 'Touch not mine anointed,
   and do my prophets no harm.'
¹⁶ Moreover he called for a famine upon the land:
   he brake the whole staff of bread.
¹⁷ He sent a man before them,
   even Joseph, who was sold for a servant,
¹⁸ whose feet they hurt with fetters:
   he was laid in iron:
¹⁹ until the time that his word came:

the word of the Lord tried him.
²⁰ The king sent and loosed him;
    even the ruler of the people, and let him go free.
²¹ He made him lord of his house,
    and ruler of all his substance:
²² to bind his princes at his pleasure;
    and teach his senators wisdom.
²³ Israel also came into Egypt;
    and Jacob sojourned in the land of Ham.
²⁴ And he increased his people greatly;
    and made them stronger than their enemies.
²⁵ He turned their heart to hate his people,
    to deal subtilly with his servants.
²⁶ He sent Moses his servant;
    and Aaron whom he had chosen.
²⁷ They shewed his signs among them,
    and wonders in the land of Ham.
²⁸ He sent darkness, and made it dark;
    and they rebelled not against his word.
²⁹ He turned their waters into blood,
    and slew their fish.
³⁰ Their land brought forth frogs in abundance,
    in the chambers of their kings.
³¹ He spake, and there came divers sorts of flies,
    and lice in all their coasts.
³² He gave them hail for rain,
    and flaming fire in their land.
³³ He smote their vines also and their fig trees;

and brake the trees of their coasts.
³⁴ He spake, and the locusts came,
and caterpillers, and that without number,
³⁵ and did eat up all the herbs in their land,
and devoured the fruit of their ground.
³⁶ He smote also all the firstborn in their land,
the chief of all their strength.
³⁷ He brought them forth also with silver and gold;
and there was not one feeble person
among their tribes.
³⁸ Egypt was glad when they departed,
for the fear of them fell upon them.
³⁹ He spread a cloud for a covering;
and fire to give light in the night.
⁴⁰ The people asked, and he brought quails,
and satisfied them with the bread of heaven.
⁴¹ He opened the rock, and the waters gushed out;
they ran in the dry places like a river.
⁴² For he remembered his holy promise,
and Abraham his servant.
⁴³ And he brought forth his people with joy,
and his chosen with gladness;
⁴⁴ and gave them the lands of the heathen;
and they inherited the labour of the people;
⁴⁵ that they might observe his statutes,
and keep his laws. Praise ye the Lord.

107

O Give thanks unto the Lord,
for he is good, for his mercy endureth for ever.

²Let the redeemed of the Lord say so,
whom he hath redeemed from the hand
of the enemy;

³and gathered them out of the lands,
from the east, and from the west,
from the north, and from the south.

⁴They wandered in the wilderness in a solitary way;
they found no city to dwell in.

⁵Hungry and thirsty,
their soul fainted in them.

⁶Then they cried unto the Lord in their trouble,
and he delivered them out of their distresses.

⁷And he led them forth by the right way,
that they might go to a city of habitation.

⁸Oh that men would praise the Lord
for his goodness,
and for his wonderful works
to the children of men!

⁹For he satisfieth the longing soul,
and filleth the hungry soul with goodness.

¹⁰Such as sit in darkness and in the shadow of death,
being bound in affliction and iron,

¹¹because they rebelled against the words of God,
and contemned the counsel of the most High;

¹²therefore he brought down their heart with labour;
they fell down, and there was none to help.

¹³ Then they cried unto the Lord in their trouble,
  and he saved them out of their distresses.
¹⁴ He brought them out of darkness
  and the shadow of death,
    and brake their bands in sunder.
¹⁵ Oh that men would praise the Lord
  for his goodness, and for his wonderful works
    to the children of men!
¹⁶ For he hath broken the gates of brass,
  and cut the bars of iron in sunder.
¹⁷ Fools because of their transgression,
  and because of their iniquities, are afflicted.
¹⁸ Their soul abhorreth all manner of meat;
  and they draw near unto the gates of death.
¹⁹ Then they cry unto the Lord in their trouble,
  and he saveth them out of their distresses.
²⁰ He sent his word, and healed them,
  and delivered them from their destructions.
²¹ Oh that men would praise the Lord
  for his goodness, and for his wonderful works
    to the children of men!
²² And let them sacrifice the sacrifices
  of thanksgiving,
    and declare his works with rejoicing.
²³ They that go down to the sea in ships,
  that do business in great waters;
²⁴ these see the works of the Lord,
  and his wonders in the deep.

²⁵ For he commandeth, and raiseth the stormy wind,
   which lifteth up the waves thereof.
²⁶ They mount up to the heaven,
   they go down again to the depths:
      their soul is melted because of trouble.
²⁷ They reel to and fro, and stagger
   like a drunken man, and are at their wits' end.
²⁸ Then they cry unto the Lord in their trouble,
   and he bringeth them out of their distresses.
²⁹ He maketh the storm a calm,
   so that the waves thereof are still.
³⁰ Then are they glad because they be quiet;
   so he bringeth them unto their desired haven.
³¹ Oh that men would praise the Lord
   for his goodness, and for his wonderful works
      to the children of men!
³² Let them exalt him also in the congregation
   of the people, and praise him
      in the assembly of the elders.
³³ He turneth rivers into a wilderness,
   and the watersprings into dry ground,
³⁴ a fruitful land into barrenness,
   for the wickedness of them that dwell therein.
³⁵ He turneth the wilderness into a standing water,
   and dry ground into watersprings.
³⁶ And there he maketh the hungry to dwell,
   that they may prepare a city for habitation,
³⁷ and sow the fields, and plant vineyards,

which may yield fruits of increase.
³⁸ He blesseth them also,
    so that they are multiplied greatly;
        and suffereth not their cattle to decrease.
³⁹ Again, they are minished and brought low
    through oppression, affliction, and sorrow.
⁴⁰ He poureth contempt upon princes,
    and causeth them to wander in the wilderness,
        where there is no way.
⁴¹ Yet setteth he the poor on high from affliction,
    and maketh him families like a flock.
⁴² The righteous shall see it, and rejoice;
    and all inquity shall stop her mouth.
⁴³ Whoso is wise, and will observe these things,
    even they shall understand the lovingkindness
        of the Lord.

111   Praise ye the Lord.
        I will praise the Lord with my whole heart,
            in the assembly of the upright,
        and in the congregation.
² The works of the Lord are great, sought out
    of all them that have pleasure therein.
³ His work is honourable and glorious;
    and his righteousness endureth for ever.
⁴ He hath made his wonderful works
    to be remembered:

the Lord is gracious and full of compassion.
⁵ He hath given meat unto them that fear him:
    he will ever be mindful of his covenant.
⁶ He hath shewed his people the power of his works,
    that he may give them the heritage
    of the heathen.
⁷ The works of his hands are verity and judgment;
    all his commandments are sure.
⁸ They stand fast for ever and ever,
    and are done in truth and uprightness.
⁹ He sent redemption unto his people:
    he hath commanded his covenant for ever:
        holy and reverend is his name.
¹⁰ The fear of the Lord is the beginning of wisdom:
    a good understanding have all they
        that do his commandments:
    his praise endureth for ever.

113

Praise ye the Lord.
    Praise, O ye servants of the Lord,
        praise the name of the Lord.
² Blessed be the name of the Lord
    from this time forth and for evermore.
³ From the rising of the sun unto the going down
    of the same the Lord's name is to be praised.
⁴ The Lord is high above all nations,
    and his glory above the heavens.

⁵ Who is like unto the Lord our God,
   who dwelleth on high,
⁶ who humbleth himself to behold the things
   that are in heaven, and in the earth!
⁷ He raiseth up the poor out of the dust,
   and lifteth the needy out of the dunghill,
⁸ that he may set him with princes,
   even with the princes of his people.
⁹ He maketh the barren woman to keep house,
   and to be a joyful mother of children.
      Praise ye the Lord.

115   Not unto us, O Lord, not unto us,
      but unto thy name give glory, for thy mercy,
         and for thy truth's sake.
² Wherefore should the heathen say,
   'Where is now their God?'
³ But our God is in the heavens:
   he hath done whatsoever he hath pleased.
⁴ Their idols are silver and gold,
   the work of men's hands.
⁵ They have mouths, but they speak not:
   eyes have they, but they see not:
⁶ they have ears, but they hear not:
   noses have they, but they smell not:
⁷ they have hands, but they handle not:
   feet have they, but they walk not:

neither speak they through their throat.
⁸ They that make them are like unto them;
    so is every one that trusteth in them.
⁹ O Israel, trust thou in the Lord:
    he is their help and their shield.
¹⁰ O house of Aaron, trust in the Lord:
    he is their help and their shield.
¹¹ Ye that fear the Lord; trust in the Lord:
    he is their help and their shield.
¹² The Lord hath been mindful of us:
    he will bless us;
        he will bless the house of Israel;
    he will bless the house of Aaron.
¹³ He will bless them that fear the Lord,
    both small and great.
¹⁴ The Lord shall increase you more and more,
    you and your children.
¹⁵ Ye are blessed of the Lord
    which made heaven and earth.
¹⁶ The heaven, even the heavens, are the Lord's:
    but the earth hath he given to the children
    of men.
¹⁷ The dead praise not the Lord,
    neither any that go down into silence.
¹⁸ But we will bless the Lord from this time forth
    and for evermore. Praise the Lord.

116 I love the Lord, because he hath heard
my voice and my supplications.

2 Because he hath inclined his ear unto me,
therefore will I call upon him as long as I live.

3 The sorrows of death compassed me,
and the pains of hell gat hold upon me:
I found trouble and sorrow.

4 Then called I upon the name of the Lord:
'O Lord, I beseech thee, deliver my soul.'

5 Gracious is the Lord, and righteous;
yea, our God is merciful.

6 The Lord preserveth the simple:
I was brought low, and he helped me.

7 Return unto thy rest, O my soul;
for the Lord hath dealt bountifully with thee.

8 For thou hast delivered my soul from death,
mine eyes from tears, and my feet from falling.

9 I will walk before the Lord
in the land of the living.

10 I believed, therefore have I spoken:
I was greatly afflicted:

11 I said in my haste, 'All men are liars.'

12 What shall I render unto the Lord
for all his benefits toward me?

13 I will take the cup of salvation,
and call upon the name of the Lord.

14 I will pay my vows unto the Lord
now in the presence of all his people.

¹⁵ Precious in the sight of the Lord
　　is the death of his saints.
¹⁶ O Lord, truly I am thy servant;
　　I am thy servant, and the son of thine handmaid:
　　　thou hast loosed my bonds.
¹⁷ I will offer to thee the sacrifice of thanksgiving,
　　and will call upon the name of the Lord.
¹⁸ I will pay my vows unto the Lord,
　　now in the presence of all his people,
¹⁹ in the courts of the Lord's house,
　　in the midst of thee, O Jerusalem.
　　　Praise ye the Lord.

117　O praise the Lord, all ye nations:
　　praise him, all ye people.
² For his merciful kindness is great toward us:
　　and the truth of the Lord endureth for ever.
　　　Praise ye the Lord.

118　O give thanks unto the Lord; for he is good,
　　because his mercy endureth for ever.
² Let Israel now say
　　that his mercy endureth for ever.
³ Let the house of Aaron now say
　　that his mercy endureth for ever.
⁴ Let them now that fear the Lord say
　　that his mercy endureth for ever.

⁵ I called upon the Lord in distress:
  the Lord answered me,
    and set me in a large place.
⁶ The Lord is on my side;
  I will not fear: what can man do unto me?
⁷ The Lord taketh my part with them that help me;
  therefore shall I see my desire
    upon them that hate me.
⁸ It is better to trust in the Lord
  than to put confidence in man.
⁹ It is better to trust in the Lord
  than to put confidence in princes.
¹⁰ All nations compassed me about;
  but in the name of the Lord will I destroy them.
¹¹ They compassed me about;
  yea, they compassed me about;
    but in the name of the Lord I will destroy
  them.
¹² They compassed me about like bees;
  they are quenched as the fire of thorns,
    for in the name of the Lord
  I will destroy them.
¹³ Thou hast thrust sore at me that I might fall;
  but the Lord helped me.
¹⁴ The Lord is my strength and song,
  and is become my salvation.
¹⁵ The voice of rejoicing and salvation is in the
  tabernacles of the righteous:

the right hand of the Lord doeth valiantly.

¹⁶ The right hand of the Lord is exalted:
   the right hand of the Lord doeth valiantly.

¹⁷ I shall not die, but live,
   and declare the works of the Lord.

¹⁸ The Lord hath chastened me sore;
   but he hath not given me over unto death.

¹⁹ Open to me the gates of righteousness:
   I will go into them, and I will praise the Lord:

²⁰ this gate of the Lord, into which
   the righteous shall enter.

²¹ I will praise thee; for thou hast heard me,
   and art become my salvation.

²² The stone which the builders refused
   is become the head stone of the corner.

²³ This is the Lord's doing;
   it is marvellous in our eyes.

²⁴ This is the day which the Lord hath made;
   we will rejoice and be glad in it.

²⁵ Save now, I beseech thee, O Lord:
   O Lord, I beseech thee, send now prosperity.

²⁶ Blessed be he that cometh in the name of the Lord:
   we have blessed you out of the house of the Lord.

²⁷ God is the Lord, which hath shewed us light:
   bind the sacrifice with cords, even unto the horns
      of the altar.

²⁸ Thou art my God, and I will praise thee:
   thou art my God, I will exalt thee.

²⁹ O give thanks unto the Lord; for he is good;
for his mercy endureth for ever.

119

ALEPH

Blessed are the undefiled in the way,
who walk in the law of the Lord.
² Blessed are they that keep his testimonies,
and that seek him with the whole heart.
³ They also do no iniquity: they walk in his ways.
⁴ Thou hast commanded us to keep
thy precepts diligently.
⁵ O that my ways were directed to keep thy statutes!
⁶ Then shall I not be ashamed,
when I have respect unto all thy commandments.
⁷ I will praise thee with uprightness of heart,
when I shall have learned
thy righteous judgments.
⁸ I will keep thy statutes;
O forsake me not utterly.

BETH

⁹ Wherewithal shall a young man cleanse his way?
By taking heed thereto according to thy word.
¹⁰ With my whole heart have I sought thee;
O let me not wander from thy commandments.
¹¹ Thy word have I hid in mine heart,
that I might not sin against thee.

¹² Blessed art thou, O Lord: teach me thy statutes.
¹³ With my lips have I declared
all the judgments of thy mouth.
¹⁴ I have rejoiced in the way of thy testimonies,
as much as in all riches.
¹⁵ I will meditate in thy precepts,
and have respect unto thy ways.
¹⁶ I will delight myself in thy statutes;
I will not forget thy word.

GIMEL

¹⁷ Deal bountifully with thy servant,
that I may live, and keep thy word.
¹⁸ Open thou mine eyes, that I may behold
wondrous things out of thy law.
¹⁹ I am a stranger in the earth:
hide not thy commandments from me.
²⁰ My soul breaketh for the longing that it hath unto
thy judgments at all times.
²¹ Thou hast rebuked the proud that are cursed,
which do err from thy commandments.
²² Remove from me reproach and contempt,
for I have kept thy testimonies.
²³ Princes also did sit and speak against me;
but thy servant did meditate in thy statutes.
²⁴ Thy testimonies also are my delight
and my counsellors.

DALETH

25 My soul cleaveth unto the dust;
  quicken thou me according to thy word.

26 I have declared my ways, and thou heardest me:
  teach me thy statutes.

27 Make me to understand the way of thy precepts;
  so shall I talk of thy wondrous works.

28 My soul melteth for heaviness:
  strengthen thou me according unto thy word.

29 Remove from me the way of lying;
  and grant me thy law graciously.

30 I have chosen the way of truth:
  thy judgments have I laid before me.

31 I have stuck unto thy testimonies:
  O Lord, put me not to shame.

32 I will run the way of thy commandments,
  when thou shalt enlarge my heart.

HE

33 Teach me, O Lord, the way of thy statutes;
  and I shall keep it unto the end.

34 Give me understanding, and I shall keep thy law;
  yea, I shall observe it with my whole heart.

35 Make me to go in the path of thy commandments;
  for therein do I delight.

36 Incline my heart unto thy testimonies,
  and not to covetousness.

³⁷ Turn away mine eyes from beholding vanity;
and quicken thou me in thy way.
³⁸ Stablish thy word unto thy servant,
who is devoted to thy fear.
³⁹ Turn away my reproach which I fear;
for thy judgments are good.
⁴⁰ Behold, I have longed after thy precepts:
quicken me in thy righteousness.

VAU

⁴¹ Let thy mercies come also unto me, O Lord,
even thy salvation, according to thy word.
⁴² So shall I have wherewith to answer him
that reproacheth me; for I trust in thy word.
⁴³ And take not the word of truth utterly
out of my mouth;
for I have hoped in thy judgments.
⁴⁴ So shall I keep thy law continually
for ever and ever.
⁴⁵ And I will walk at liberty; for I seek thy precepts.
⁴⁶ I will speak of thy testimonies also before kings,
and will not be ashamed.
⁴⁷ And I will delight myself in thy commandments,
which I have loved.
⁴⁸ My hands also will I lift up
unto thy commandments, which I have loved;
and I will meditate in thy statutes.

ZAIN

⁴⁹ Remember the word unto thy servant,
  upon which thou hast caused me to hope.
⁵⁰ This is my comfort in my affliction;
  for thy word hath quickened me.
⁵¹ The proud have had me greatly in derision;
  yet have I not declined from thy law.
⁵² I remembered thy judgments of old, O Lord;
  and have comforted myself.
⁵³ Horror hath taken hold upon me
  because of the wicked that forsake thy law.
⁵⁴ Thy statutes have been my songs
  in the house of my pilgrimage.
⁵⁵ I have remembered thy name, O Lord,
  in the night, and have kept thy law.
⁵⁶ This I had, because I kept thy precepts.

CHETH

⁵⁷ Thou art my portion, O Lord:
  I have said that I would keep thy words.
⁵⁸ I intreated thy favour with my whole heart:
  be merciful unto me according to thy word.
⁵⁹ I thought on my ways,
  and turned my feet unto thy testimonies.
⁶⁰ I made haste,
  and delayed not to keep thy commandments.
⁶¹ The bands of the wicked have robbed me;
  but I have not forgotten thy law.

⁶²At midnight I will rise to give thanks unto thee
    because of thy righteous judgments.
⁶³I am a companion of all them that fear thee,
    and of them that keep thy precepts.
⁶⁴The earth, O Lord, is full of thy mercy:
    teach me thy statutes.

TETH

⁶⁵Thou hast dealt well with thy servant, O Lord,
    according unto thy word.
⁶⁶Teach me good judgment and knowledge;
    for I have believed thy commandments.
⁶⁷Before I was afflicted I went astray;
    but now have I kept thy word.
⁶⁸Thou art good, and doest good;
    teach me thy statutes.
⁶⁹The proud have forged a lie against me;
    but I will keep thy precepts with my whole heart.
⁷⁰Their heart is as fat as grease;
    but I delight in thy law.
⁷¹It is good for me that I have been afflicted;
    that I might learn thy statutes.
⁷²The law of thy mouth is better unto me
    than thousands of gold and silver.

JOD

⁷³Thy hands have made me and fashioned me:
    give me understanding,
        that I may learn thy commandments.

⁷⁴ They that fear thee will be glad when they see me;
    because I have hoped in thy word.
⁷⁵ I know, O Lord, that thy judgments are right,
    and that thou in faithfulness hast afflicted me.
⁷⁶ Let, I pray thee, thy merciful kindness
    be for my comfort,
        according to thy word unto thy servant.
⁷⁷ Let thy tender mercies come unto me,
    that I may live; for thy law is my delight.
⁷⁸ Let the proud be ashamed;
    for they dealt perversely with me
        without a cause;
    but I will meditate in thy precepts.
⁷⁹ Let those that fear thee turn unto me,
    and those that have known thy testimonies.
⁸⁰ Let my heart be sound in thy statutes;
    that I be not ashamed.

CAPH

⁸¹ My soul fainteth for thy salvation;
    but I hope in thy word.
⁸² Mine eyes fail for thy word, saying,
    'When wilt thou comfort me?'
⁸³ For I am become like a bottle in the smoke;
    yet do I not forget thy statutes.
⁸⁴ How many are the days of thy servant?
    When wilt thou execute judgment on them
        that persecute me?

⁸⁵ The proud have digged pits for me,
    which are not after thy law.
⁸⁶ All thy commandments are faithful;
    they persecute me wrongfully;
        help thou me.
⁸⁷ They had almost consumed me upon earth;
    but I forsook not thy precepts.
⁸⁸ Quicken me after thy lovingkindness;
    so shall I keep the testimony of thy mouth.

LAMED

⁸⁹ For ever, O Lord, thy word is settled in heaven.
⁹⁰ Thy faithfulness is unto all generations:
    thou hast established the earth, and it abideth.
⁹¹ They continue this day according to
    thine ordinances; for all are thy servants.
⁹² Unless thy law had been my delights,
    I should then have perished in mine affliction.
⁹³ I will never forget thy precepts;
    for with them thou hast quickened me.
⁹⁴ I am thine, save me;
    for I have sought thy precepts.
⁹⁵ The wicked have waited for me to destroy me;
    but I will consider thy testimonies.
⁹⁶ I have seen an end of all perfection;
    but thy commandment is exceeding broad.

MEM

⁹⁷ O how love I thy law!
  It is my meditation all the day.
⁹⁸ Thou through thy commandments hast made
    me wiser than mine enemies;
      for they are ever with me.
⁹⁹ I have more understanding than all my teachers;
    for thy testimonies are my meditation.
¹⁰⁰ I understand more than the ancients,
    because I keep thy precepts.
¹⁰¹ I have refrained my feet from every evil way,
    that I might keep thy word.
¹⁰² I have not departed from thy judgments;
    for thou hast taught me.
¹⁰³ How sweet are thy words unto my taste!
    Yea, sweeter than honey to my mouth!
¹⁰⁴ Through thy precepts I get understanding;
    therefore I hate every false way.

NUN

¹⁰⁵ Thy word is a lamp unto my feet,
    and a light unto my path.
¹⁰⁶ I have sworn, and I will perform it,
    that I will keep thy righteous judgments.
¹⁰⁷ I am afflicted very much: quicken me, O Lord,
      according unto thy word.
¹⁰⁸ Accept, I beseech thee,

the freewill offerings of my mouth, O Lord,
and teach me thy judgments.
[109] My soul is continually in my hand;
yet do I not forget thy law.
[110] The wicked have laid a snare for me;
yet I erred not from thy precepts.
[111] Thy testimonies have I taken as an heritage for ever;
for they are the rejoicing of my heart.
[112] I have inclined mine heart to perform thy statutes
alway, even unto the end.

SAMECH

[113] I hate vain thoughts; but thy law do I love.
[114] Thou art my hiding place and my shield:
I hope in thy word.
[115] Depart from me, ye evildoers;
for I will keep the commandments of my God.
[116] Uphold me according unto thy word,
that I may live;
and let me not be ashamed of my hope.
[117] Hold thou me up, and I shall be safe;
and I will have respect unto thy statutes continually.
[118] Thou hast trodden down all them that err
from thy statutes; for their deceit is falsehood.
[119] Thou puttest away all the wicked of the earth
like dross; therefore I love thy testimonies.
[120] My flesh trembleth for fear of thee;

and I am afraid of thy judgments.

AIN

¹²¹ I have done judgment and justice:
leave me not to mine oppressors.
¹²² Be surety for thy servant for good:
let not the proud oppress me.
¹²³ Mine eyes fail for thy salvation,
and for the word of thy righteousness.
¹²⁴ Deal with thy servant according unto thy mercy,
and teach me thy statutes.
¹²⁵ I am thy servant; give me understanding,
that I may know thy testimonies.
¹²⁶ It is time for thee, Lord, to work;
for they have made void thy law.
¹²⁷ Therefore I love thy commandments above gold;
yea, above fine gold.
¹²⁸ Therefore I esteem all thy precepts concerning
all things to be right;
and I hate every false way.

PE

¹²⁹ Thy testimonies are wonderful;
therefore doth my soul keep them.
¹³⁰ The entrance of thy words giveth light;
it giveth understanding unto the simple.
¹³¹ I opened my mouth, and panted;
for I longed for thy commandments.

132 Look thou upon me, and be merciful unto me,
    as thou usest to do unto those that love thy
        name.

133 Order my steps in thy word;
    and let not any iniquity have dominion over
        me.

134 Deliver me from the oppression of man:
    so will I keep thy precepts.

135 Make thy face to shine upon thy servant;
    and teach me thy statutes.

136 Rivers of waters run down mine eyes,
    because they keep not thy law.

TZADDI

137 Righteous art thou, O Lord,
    and upright are thy judgments.

138 Thy testimonies that thou hast commanded
    are righteous and very faithful.

139 My zeal hath consumed me,
    because mine enemies have forgotten thy words.

140 Thy word is very pure;
    therefore thy servant loveth it.

141 I am small and despised;
    yet do not I forget thy precepts.

142 Thy righteousness is an everlasting righteousness,
    and thy law is the truth.

143 Trouble and anguish have taken hold on me;
    yet thy commandments are my delights.

[144] The righteousness of thy testimonies is everlasting:
give me understanding, and I shall live.

KOPH

[145] I cried with my whole heart;
hear me, O Lord: I will keep thy statutes.
[146] I cried unto thee;
save me, and I shall keep thy testimonies.
[147] I prevented the dawning of the morning,
and cried: 'I hoped in thy word.'
[148] Mine eyes prevent the night watches,
that I might meditate in thy word.
[149] Hear my voice according unto thy lovingkindness:
'O Lord, quicken me according to thy judgment.'
[150] They draw nigh that follow after mischief:
they are far from thy law.
[151] Thou art near, O Lord;
and all thy commandments are truth.
[152] Concerning thy testimonies,
I have known of old that thou hast founded
them for ever.

RESH

[153] Consider mine affliction, and deliver me;
for I do not forget thy law.
[154] Plead my cause, and deliver me:
quicken me according to thy word.
[155] Salvation is far from the wicked;

for they seek not thy statutes.

¹⁵⁶ Great are thy tender mercies, O Lord:
quicken me according to thy judgments.

¹⁵⁷ Many are my persecutors and mine enemies;
yet do I not decline from thy testimonies.

¹⁵⁸ I beheld the transgressors, and was grieved;
because they kept not thy word.

¹⁵⁹ Consider how I love thy precepts:
quicken me, O Lord, according to thy
lovingkindness.

¹⁶⁰ Thy word is true from the beginning;
and every one of thy righteous judgments
endureth for ever.

SCHIN

¹⁶¹ Princes have persecuted me without a cause;
but my heart standeth in awe of thy word.

¹⁶² I rejoice at thy word,
as one that findeth great spoil.

¹⁶³ I hate and abhor lying;
but thy law do I love.

¹⁶⁴ Seven times a day do I praise thee
because of thy righteous judgments.

¹⁶⁵ Great peace have they which love thy law;
and nothing shall offend them.

¹⁶⁶ Lord, I have hoped for thy salvation,
and done thy commandments.

¹⁶⁷ My soul hath kept thy testimonies;

and I love them exceedingly.

¹⁶⁸ I have kept thy precepts and thy testimonies;
for all my ways are before thee.

TAU

¹⁶⁹ Let my cry come near before thee, O Lord:
give me understanding according to thy word.

¹⁷⁰ Let my supplication come before thee:
deliver me according to thy word.

¹⁷¹ My lips shall utter praise,
when thou hast taught me thy statutes.

¹⁷² My tongue shall speak of thy word;
for all thy commandments are righteousness.

¹⁷³ Let thine hand help me;
for I have chosen thy precepts.

¹⁷⁴ I have longed for thy salvation, O Lord;
and thy law is my delight.

¹⁷⁵ Let my soul live, and it shall praise thee;
and let thy judgments help me.

¹⁷⁶ I have gone astray like a lost sheep;
seek thy servant;

for I do not forget thy commandments.

121

A song of degrees.

I will lift up mine eyes unto the hills,
from whence cometh my help.

² My help cometh from the Lord,

which made heaven and earth.
³ He will not suffer thy foot to be moved:
   he that keepeth thee will not slumber.
⁴ Behold, he that keepeth Israel shall neither
   slumber nor sleep.
⁵ The Lord is thy keeper:
   the Lord is thy shade upon thy right hand.
⁶ The sun shall not smite thee by day,
   nor the moon by night.
⁷ The Lord shall preserve thee from all evil:
   he shall preserve thy soul.
⁸ The Lord shall preserve thy going out
   and thy coming in from this time forth,
      and even for evermore.

122

A song of degrees of David.

I was glad when they said unto me,
   'Let us go into the house of the Lord.'
² Our feet shall stand within thy gates,
   O Jerusalem.
³ Jerusalem is builded as a city
   that is compact together.
⁴ Whither the tribes go up, the tribes of the Lord,
   unto the testimony of Israel,
      to give thanks unto the name of the Lord.
⁵ For there are set thrones of judgment,
   the thrones of the house of David.

⁶ Pray for the peace of Jerusalem:
  they shall prosper that love thee.
⁷ Peace be within thy walls,
  and prosperity within thy palaces.
⁸ For my brethren and companions' sakes,
  I will now say, 'Peace be within thee.'
⁹ Because of the house of the Lord our God
  I will seek thy good.

124   A song of degrees of David.

  If it had not been the Lord who was on our side,
    now may Israel say;
² if it had not been the Lord who was on our side,
    when men rose up against us,
³ then they had swallowed us up quick,
    when their wrath was kindled against us;
⁴ then the waters had overwhelmed us,
    the stream had gone over our soul;
⁵ then the proud waters had gone over our soul.
⁶ Blessed be the Lord,
    who hath not given us as a prey to their teeth.
⁷ Our soul is escaped as a bird out of the snare
    of the fowlers:
      the snare is broken, and we are escaped.
⁸ Our help is in the name of the Lord,
    who made heaven and earth.

126

A song of degrees.

When the Lord turned again the captivity of Zion,
we were like them that dream.
² Then was our mouth filled with laughter,
and our tongue with singing;
then said they among the heathen,
'The Lord hath done great things for them.'
³ The Lord hath done great things for us;
whereof we are glad.
⁴ Turn again our captivity, O Lord,
as the streams in the south.
⁵ They that sow in tears shall reap in joy.
⁶ He that goeth forth and weepeth,
bearing precious seed,
shall doubtless come again with rejoicing,
bringing his sheaves with him.

127

A song of degrees for Solomon.

Except the Lord build the house,
they labour in vain that build it;
except the Lord keep the city,
the watchman waketh but in vain.
² It is vain for you to rise up early,
to sit up late, to eat the bread of sorrows;
for so he giveth his beloved sleep.
³ Lo, children are an heritage of the Lord;
and the fruit of the womb is his reward.

⁴As arrows are in the hand of a mighty man;
　　so are children of the youth.
⁵Happy is the man that hath his quiver full of them:
　　they shall not be ashamed,
　　　　but they shall speak with the enemies
　　in the gate.

128　A song of degrees.

Blessed is every one that feareth the Lord;
　　that walketh in his ways.
²For thou shalt eat the labour of thine hands:
　　happy shalt thou be,
　　and it shall be well with thee.
³Thy wife shall be as a fruitful vine by the sides
　　of thine house: thy children like olive plants
　　　　round about thy table.
⁴Behold, that thus shall the man be blessed
　　that feareth the Lord.
⁵The Lord shall bless thee out of Zion;
　　and thou shalt see the good of Jerusalem
　　　　all the days of thy life.
⁶Yea, thou shalt see thy children's children,
　　and peace upon Israel.

130　A song of degrees.

Out of the depths have I cried unto thee, O Lord.

² Lord, hear my voice: let thine ears be attentive
      to the voice of my supplications.
³ If thou, Lord, shouldest mark inquities,
      O Lord, who shall stand?
⁴ But there is forgiveness with thee,
      that thou mayest be feared.
⁵ I wait for the Lord, my soul doth wait,
      and in his word do I hope.
⁶ My soul waiteth for the Lord more than they that
      watch for the morning:
            I say, more than they that watch
      for the morning.
⁷ Let Israel hope in the Lord;
      for with the Lord there is mercy,
            and with him is plenteous redemption.
⁸ And he shall redeem Israel from all his iniquities.

133

A song of degrees of David.

Behold, how good and how pleasant it is
      for brethren to dwell together in unity!
² It is like the precious ointment upon the head,
      that ran down upon the beard,
            even Aaron's beard;
      that went down to the skirts of his garments;
³ as the dew of Hermon,
      and as the dew that descended upon
            the mountains of Zion;

for there the Lord commanded the blessing,
even life for evermore.

134

A song of degrees.

Behold, bless ye the Lord,
all ye servants of the Lord,
which by night stand in the house of the Lord.
² Lift up your hands in the sanctuary,
and bless the Lord.
³ The Lord that made heaven and earth
bless thee out of Zion.

136

O Give thanks unto the Lord; for he is good;
for his mercy endureth for ever.
² O give thanks unto the God of gods;
for his mercy endureth for ever.
³ O give thanks to the Lord of lords;
for his mercy endureth for ever.
⁴ To him who alone doeth great wonders;
for his mercy endureth for ever.
⁵ To him that by wisdom made the heavens;
for his mercy endureth for ever.
⁶ To him that stretched out the earth
above the waters;
for his mercy endureth for ever.
⁷ To him that made great lights;

for his mercy endureth for ever:
8 the sun to rule by day;
for his mercy endureth for ever:
9 the moon and stars to rule by night;
for his mercy endureth for ever.
10 To him that smote Egypt in their firstborn;
for his mercy endureth for ever;
11 and brought out Israel from among them;
for his mercy endureth for ever;
12 with a strong hand, and with a stretched out arm;
for his mercy endureth for ever.
13 To him which divided the Red sea into parts;
for his mercy endureth for ever;
14 and made Israel to pass through the midst of it;
for his mercy endureth for ever;
15 but overthrew Pharaoh and his host in the Red sea;
for his mercy endureth for ever.
16 To him which led his people
through the wilderness;
for his mercy endureth for ever.
17 To him which smote great kings;
for his mercy endureth for ever;
18 and slew famous kings;
for his mercy endureth for ever;
19 Sihon king of the Amorites;
for his mercy endureth for ever;
20 and Og the king of Bashan;
for his mercy endureth for ever;
21 and gave their land for an heritage;

for his mercy endureth for ever;
²² even an heritage unto Israel his servant;
for his mercy endureth for ever.
²³ Who remembered us in our low estate;
for his mercy endureth for ever;
²⁴ and hath redeemed us from our enemies;
for his mercy endureth for ever.
²⁵ Who giveth food to all flesh;
for his mercy endureth for ever.
²⁶ O give thanks unto the God of heaven;
for his mercy endureth for ever.

137   By the rivers of Babylon, there we sat down,
yea, we wept, when we remembered Zion.
² We hanged our harps upon the willows
in the midst thereof.
³ For there they that carried us away captive
required of us a song;
and they that wasted us required of us mirth,
saying, 'Sing us one of the songs of Zion.'
⁴ How shall we sing the Lord's song
in a strange land?
⁵ If I forget thee, O Jerusalem,
let my right hand forget her cunning.
⁶ If I do not remember thee,
let my tongue cleave to the roof of my mouth;
if I prefer not Jerusalem above my chief joy.

⁷ Remember, O Lord,
  the children of Edom in the day of Jerusalem;
    who said, 'Rase it, rase it,
  even to the foundation thereof.'
⁸ O daughter of Babylon, who art to be destroyed;
  happy shall he be, that rewardeth thee
    as thou hast served us.
⁹ Happy shall he be,
  that taketh and dasheth thy little ones
    against the stones.

138 A psalm of David.

I will praise thee with my whole heart:
  before the gods will I sing praise unto thee.
² I will worship toward thy holy temple,
  and praise thy name for thy loving-kindness
    and for thy truth;
  for thou hast magnified thy word above
    all thy name.
³ In the day when I cried thou answeredst me,
  and strengthenedst me with strength
    in my soul.
⁴ All the kings of the earth shall praise thee, O Lord,
  when they hear the words of thy mouth.
⁵ Yea, they shall sing in the ways of the Lord;
  for great is the glory of the Lord.
⁶ Though the Lord be high,

yet hath he respect unto the lowly;
  but the proud he knoweth afar off.
⁷ Though I walk in the midst of trouble,
  thou wilt revive me;
   thou shalt stretch forth thine hand
  against the wrath of mine enemies,
   and thy right hand shall save me.
⁸ The Lord will perfect that which concerneth me:
  thy mercy, O Lord, endureth for ever:
   forsake not the works of thine own hands.

139

To the chief musician, a psalm of David.

O Lord, thou hast searched me, and known me.
² Thou knowest my downsitting and mine uprising,
  thou understandest my thought afar off.
³ Thou compassest my path and my lying down,
  and art acquainted with all my ways.
⁴ For there is not a word in my tongue,
  but, lo, O Lord, thou knowest it altogether.
⁵ Thou hast beset me behind and before,
  and laid thine hand upon me.
⁶ Such knowledge is too wonderful for me;
  it is high, I cannot attain unto it.
⁷ Whither shall I go from thy spirit?
  Or whither shall I flee from thy presence?
⁸ If I ascend up into heaven, thou art there:
  if I make my bed in hell, behold, thou art there.

⁹ If I take the wings of the morning,
 and dwell in the uttermost parts of the sea;
¹⁰ even there shall thy hand lead me,
 and thy right hand shall hold me.
¹¹ If I say, 'Surely the darkness shall cover me;
 even the night shall be light about me.'
¹² Yea, the darkness hideth not from thee;
 but the night shineth as the day;
  the darkness and the light are both
 alike to thee.
¹³ For thou hast possessed my reins:
 thou hast covered me in my mother's womb.
¹⁴ I will praise thee;
 for I am fearfully and wonderfully made;
  marvellous are thy works;
 and that my soul knoweth right well.
¹⁵ My substance was not hid from thee,
 when I was made in secret,
  and curiously wrought in the lowest parts
 of the earth.
¹⁶ Thine eyes did see my substance,
 yet being unperfect; and in thy book
 all my members were written,
  which in continuance were fashioned when
 as yet there was none of them.
¹⁷ How precious also are thy thoughts unto me,
 O God! How great is the sum of them!
¹⁸ If I should count them, they are more in number

than the sand:
>> when I awake, I am still with thee.

19 Surely thou wilt slay the wicked, O God:
>> depart from me therefore, ye bloody men.

20 For they speak against thee wickedly,
>> and thine enemies take thy name in vain.

21 Do not I hate them, O Lord, that hate thee?
>> And am not I grieved with those that rise up
>> against thee?

22 I hate them with perfect hatred:
>> I count them mine enemies.

23 Search me, O God, and know my heart:
>> try me, and know my thoughts:

24 and see if there be any wicked way in me,
>> and lead me in the way everlasting.

141

A psalm of David.

Lord, I cry unto thee: make haste unto me;
>> give ear unto my voice, when I cry unto thee.

2 Let my prayer be set forth before thee as incense;
>> and the lifting up of my hands
>> as the evening sacrifice.

3 Set a watch, O Lord, before my mouth;
>> keep the door of my lips.

4 Incline not my heart to any evil thing,
>> to practise wicked works with men
>> that work iniquity;

and let me not eat of their dainties.
⁵ Let the righteous smite me;
it shall be a kindness; and let him reprove me;
it shall be an excellent oil,
which shall not break my head;
for yet my prayer also shall be in their calami-
ties.
⁶ When their judges are overthrown in stony places,
they shall hear my words; for they are sweet.
⁷ Our bones are scattered at the grave's mouth,
as when one cutteth and cleaveth wood
upon the earth.
⁸ But mine eyes are unto thee, O God the Lord:
in thee is my trust; leave not my soul destitute.
⁹ Keep me from the snares
which they have laid for me,
and the gins of the workers of iniquity.
¹⁰ Let the wicked fall into their own nets,
whilst that I withal escape.

142 Maschil of David; a prayer when he was
in the cave.

I cried unto the Lord with my voice;
with my voice unto the Lord
did I make my supplication.
² I poured out my complaint before him;
I shewed before him my trouble.

³ When my spirit was overwhelmed within me,
then thou knewest my path.
  In the way wherein I walked
have they privily laid a snare for me.
⁴ I looked on my right hand, and beheld,
but there was no man that would know me;
  refuge failed me;
no man cared for my soul.
⁵ I cried unto thee, O Lord; I said,
  'Thou art my refuge and my portion
in the land of the living.'
⁶ Attend unto my cry; for I am brought very low;
  deliver me from my persecutors;
for they are stronger than I.
⁷ Bring my soul out of prison, that I may praise
thy name;
  the righteous shall compass me about;
for thou shalt deal bountifully with me.

143   A psalm of David.

Hear my prayer, O Lord,
  give ear to my supplications:
in thy faithfulness answer me,
  and in thy righteousness.
² And enter not into judgment with thy servant;
  for in thy sight shall no man living
be justified.

³ For the enemy hath persecuted my soul;
    he hath smitten my life down to the ground;
        he hath made me to dwell in darkness,
    as those that have been long dead.
⁴ Therefore is my spirit overwhelmed within me;
    my heart within me is desolate.
⁵ I remember the days of old;
    I meditate on all thy works;
        I muse on the work of thy hands.
⁶ I stretch forth my hands unto thee:
    my soul thirsteth after thee,
        as a thirsty land. Selah.
⁷ Hear me speedily, O Lord: my spirit faileth:
        hide not thy face from me, lest I be like unto
    them that go down into the pit.
⁸ Cause me to hear thy lovingkindness in
    the morning; for in thee do I trust:
        cause me to know the way wherein
    I should walk; for I lift up my soul unto thee.
⁹ Deliver me, O Lord, from mine enemies:
    I flee unto thee to hide me.
¹⁰ Teach me to do thy will;
    for thou art my God: thy spirit is good;
        lead me into the land of uprightness.
¹¹ Quicken me, O Lord, for thy name's sake;
        for thy righteousness' sake bring my soul
    out of trouble.
¹² And of thy mercy cut off mine enemies,

and destroy all them that afflict my soul;
  for I am thy servant.

145

David's psalm of praise.

I will extol thee, my God, O king;
  and I will bless thy name for ever and ever.
[2] Every day will I bless thee;
  and I will praise thy name for ever and ever.
[3] Great is the Lord, and greatly to be praised;
  and his greatness is unsearchable.
[4] One generation shall praise thy works to another,
  and shall declare thy mighty acts.
[5] I will speak of the glorious honour of thy majesty,
  and of thy wondrous works.
[6] And men shall speak of the might
    of thy terrible acts;
      and I will declare thy greatness.
[7] They shall abundantly utter the memory
    of thy great goodness,
      and shall sing of thy righteousness.
[8] The Lord is gracious, and full of compassion;
    slow to anger, and of great mercy.
[9] The Lord is good to all;
  and his tender mercies are over all his works.
[10] All thy works shall praise thee, O Lord;
  and thy saints shall bless thee.
[11] They shall speak of the glory of thy kingdom,

and talk of thy power;
12 to make known to the sons of men his mighty acts,
and the glorious majesty of his kingdom.
13 Thy kingdom is an everlasting kingdom,
and thy dominion endureth throughout
all generations.
14 The Lord upholdeth all that fall,
and raiseth up all those that be bowed down.
15 The eyes of all wait upon thee;
and thou givest them their meat in due season.
16 Thou openest thine hand,
and satisfiest the desire of every living thing.
17 The Lord is righteous in all his ways,
and holy in all his works.
18 The Lord is nigh unto all them that call upon him,
to all that call upon him in truth.
19 He will fulfil the desire of them that fear him;
he also will hear their cry, and will save them.
20 The Lord preserveth all them that love him;
but all the wicked will he destroy.
21 My mouth shall speak the praise of the Lord;
and let all flesh bless his holy name
for ever and ever.

146

Praise ye the Lord. Praise the Lord, O my soul.
2 While I live will I praise the Lord:
I will sing praises unto my God while I have

any being.

³ Put not your trust in princes, nor in
    the son of man, in whom there is no help.
⁴ His breath goeth forth, he returneth to his earth;
    in that very day his thoughts perish.
⁵ Happy is he that hath the God of Jacob for his help,
    whose hope is in the Lord his God,
⁶ which made heaven, and earth, the sea,
    and all that therein is;
        which keepeth truth for ever;
⁷ which executeth judgment for the oppressed;
    which giveth food to the hungry.
        The Lord looseth the prisoners.
⁸ The Lord openeth the eyes of the blind;
    the Lord raiseth them that are bowed down;
        the Lord loveth the righteous;
⁹ the Lord preserveth the strangers;
    he relieveth the fatherless and widow;
        but the way of the wicked
    he turneth upside down.
¹⁰ The Lord shall reign for ever,
    even thy God, O Zion, unto all generations.
        Praise ye the Lord.

147
    Praise ye the Lord;
        for it is good to sing praises unto our God;
    for it is pleasant; and praise is comely.

² The Lord doth build up Jerusalem:
   he gathereth together the outcasts of Israel.
³ He healeth the broken in heart,
   and bindeth up their wounds.
⁴ He telleth the number of the stars;
   he calleth them all by their names.
⁵ Great is our Lord, and of great power:
      his understanding is infinite.
⁶ The Lord lifteth up the meek:
   he casteth the wicked down to the ground.
⁷ Sing unto the Lord with thanksgiving;
   sing praise upon the harp unto our God,
⁸ who covereth the heaven with clouds,
   who prepareth rain for the earth,
      who maketh grass to grow upon
      the mountains.
⁹ He giveth to the beast his food,
   and to the young ravens which cry.
¹⁰ He delighteth not in the strength of the horse:
   he taketh not pleasure in the legs of a man.
¹¹ The Lord taketh pleasure in them that fear him,
   in those that hope in his mercy.
¹² Praise the Lord, O Jerusalem;
   praise thy God, O Zion.
¹³ For he hath strengthened the bars of thy gates;
   he hath blessed thy children within thee.
¹⁴ He maketh peace in thy borders,
   and filleth thee with the finest of the wheat.

¹⁵ He sendeth forth his commandment upon earth:
   his word runneth very swiftly.
¹⁶ He giveth snow like wool:
   he scattereth the hoarfrost like ashes.
¹⁷ He casteth forth his ice like morsels.
   Who can stand before his cold?
¹⁸ He sendeth out his word, and melteth them:
   he causeth his wind to blow, and the waters flow.
¹⁹ He sheweth his word unto Jacob,
   his statutes and his judgments unto
      Israel.
²⁰ He hath not dealt so with any nation;
   and as for his judgments,
      they have not known them.
   Praise ye the Lord.

148   Praise ye the Lord.
      Praise ye the Lord from the heavens:
   praise him in the heights.
² Praise ye him, all his angels:
   praise ye him, all his hosts.
³ Praise ye him, sun and moon:
   praise him, all ye stars of light.
⁴ Praise him, ye heavens of heavens,
   and ye waters that be above the heavens.
⁵ Let them praise the name of the Lord;
   for he commanded, and they were created.

⁶ He hath also stablished them for ever and ever:
    he hath made a decree which shall not pass.
⁷ Praise the Lord from the earth,
    ye dragons, and all deeps;
⁸ fire, and hail; snow, and vapour;
        stormy wind fulfilling his word.
⁹ Mountains, and all hills;
    fruitful trees, and all cedars;
¹⁰ beasts, and all cattle;
    creeping things, and flying fowl.
¹¹ Kings of the earth, and all people;
    princes, and all judges of the earth;
¹² both young men, and maidens;
    old men, and children.
¹³ Let them praise the name of the Lord;
    for his name alone is excellent;
        his glory is above the earth and heaven.
¹⁴ He also exalteth the horn of his people,
    the praise of all his saints;
        even of the children of Israel,
    a people near unto him. Praise ye the Lord.

149 Praise ye the Lord.
        Sing unto the Lord a new song,
    and his praise in the congregation of saints.
² Let Israel rejoice in him that made him:
    let the children of Zion be joyful in their King.

³ Let them praise his name in the dance:
   let them sing praises unto him
      with the timbrel and harp.
⁴ For the Lord taketh pleasure in his people:
   he will beautify the meek with salvation.
⁵ Let the saints be joyful in glory:
   let them sing aloud upon their beds.
⁶ Let the high praises of God be in their mouth,
   and a twoedged sword in their hand;
⁷ to execute vengeance upon the heathen,
   and punishments upon the people;
⁸ to bind their kings with chains,
   and their nobles with fetters of iron;
⁹ to execute upon them the judgment written:
   this honour have all his saints.
      Praise ye the Lord.

150   Praise ye the Lord.
      Praise God in his sanctuary:
   praise him in the firmament of his power.
² Praise him for his mighty acts:
   praise him according to his excellent greatness.
³ Praise him with the sound of the trumpet:
   praise him with the psaltery and harp.
⁴ Praise him with the timbrel and dance:
   praise him with stringed instruments and organs.
⁵ Praise him upon the loud cymbals:

praise him upon the high sounding cymbals.
[6] Let every thing that hath breath praise the Lord.
Praise ye the Lord.